# I STILL DO

### THE ULTIMATE MARRIAGE GUIDE TO HEAL, RESTORE, AND STRENGTHEN YOUR RELATIONSHIP

## JAMES BOYD

Copyright © 2025 by James Boyd

Cover Art Copyright © 2025 by David Defillipo

All rights reserved. No part of this publication may be reproduced, stored or transmitted in any form or by any means, electronic, mechanical, photocopying, recording, scanning, or otherwise without written permission from the publisher. It is illegal to copy this book, post it to a website, or distribute it by any other means without permission.

James Boyd has no responsibility for the persistence or accuracy of URLs for external or third-party Internet Websites referred to in this publication and does not guarantee that any content on such Websites is, or will remain, accurate or appropriate.

First edition

ISBN: 979-8-9904872-2-2

# CONTENTS

*Foreword* — vii
*Acknowledgements* — ix
*Introduction* — xiii

1. **Part 1** — 1
   *Meeting Expectations*

   **Chapter 1** — 3
   *The Defraudment Clause*

   Marriage Activation 1 — 9

   **Chapter 2** — 13
   *Count the Cost of Marriage*

   Marriage Activation 2 — 35

   **Chapter 3** — 37
   *If Marriage Was An Island*

   Marriage Activation 3 — 41

   **Chapter 4** — 45
   *My Job, Your Job*

   Marriage Activation 4 — 57

   **Chapter 5** — 59
   *Marriage Tune-Up*

   Marriage Activation 5 — 87

2. **Part 2** — 89
   *Covenant*

   **Chapter 6** — 91
   *The Purpose of a Covenant*

   Marriage Activation 6 — 111

   **Chapter 7** — 113
   *The Power of a Covenant*

   Marriage Activation 7 — 135

Chapter 8     137
*Sometimes It's the Little Things*

Marriage Activation 8     145

3. Part 3     147
*Communication*

Chapter 9     149
*Communication Lost*

Marriage Activation 9     165

Chapter 10     167
*I Just Want to Be Friends Again*

Marriage Activation 10     173

CHAPTER 11     177
*Becoming Faithful Stewards In Your Finances*
By Jim Weaver

Marriage Activation 11     189

CHAPTER 12     191
*Finances: Let's Get Practical*
By Jim Weaver

Marriage Activation 12     207

Chapter 13     209
*Setting the Foundation for a Godly Home*

Marriage Activation 13     229

CHAPTER 14     233
*When You're Called to Parent Someone Else's Child*
By Billy and Kristen

Marriage Activation 14     241

4. Part 4     243
*Intimacy*

Chapter 15     245
*I Own You*

Marriage Activation 15     253

Chapter 16     257
*Enough is Enough*

| | |
|---|---|
| Marriage Activation 16 | 269 |
| Chapter 17 | 271 |
| *How Many Are In Our Bed?* | |
| Marriage Activation 17 | 287 |
| Chapter 18 | 291 |
| *What Happened To The Passion?* | |
| Marriage Activation 18 | 299 |
| Let's Make a Deal | 301 |
| Further Reading | 307 |
| *A Note from the Author* | 309 |
| *Resources* | 311 |

# FOREWORD

*I Still Do* has been in the making for over thirty years. It has been in my heart to compile a resource for couples, made up of research I gathered for my thesis while I was in my Master's Program and the many years of experience in offering marriage and family counseling.

This resource is meant to be a **self-counseling tool.** There is nothing wrong with coming to a pastor or counselor to meet face-to-face when things come to an impasse, but having the tools needed to walk through marriage challenges, as well as the joys, is something that cannot be overlooked. *I Still Do* is meant to equip you as a couple to work through the things in your marriage that need to change or simply be strengthened.

In these pages, you will find a wealth of practicum but also of scripture. I am a firm believer that nothing will help a *marriage on the rocks* more than a personal touch from our Almighty God. As you begin this book, be prepared to take notes, dig into your Bible, and be open to the leading of the Holy Spirit. Without Him, the advice given might as well be just another textbook. But through the anointing and leading of the Holy Spirit, *all things are possible.*

# ACKNOWLEDGEMENTS

There are several people I would like to thank, without whom, this book would never have made it past the dream stage. Throughout this resource, you will find several contributors who have helped write different sections of the book, who I would like to recognize now.

**Pastor Jim Weaver:** Thank you for your invaluable insight and wisdom in the area of finances. Your display of God's character through your life is an inspiration to me and so many others. It is an honor to serve the Lord alongside you.

> Pastor Jim has been married to his lovely wife, Jaime, for 22 years. They have three amazing children, Lynnae, Josh, and Grace. He has been the worship pastor at Refuge City Church for over 20 years. He also handles the role as the church's finance officer, is a licensed budget coach through Ramsey Solutions, and is a published author. His debut teaching book, *Foundation Stones*, details 20 lessons on foundational principles of the Christian faith, such as water baptism and being filled with the Holy Spirit. You can find *Foundation Stones* on Amazon.

**Nicole Boyd:** My favorite daughter-in-law! (And only daughter-in-law). Thank you for all your time and hard work on this manuscript, sis! I love you with all my heart and can't wait to see all that God is doing and will do through your life. And thanks for marrying my son.

> Nicole has been married to her husband, Colton, for over twelve years. They have two children whom they adore, Kaleb and Kallie. Nicole works at Refuge City Church as the Creative Director and is Pastor Jim Weaver's personal assistant. She also helps out with the youth ministry alongside her husband who is the lead youth pastor, and their young adults discipleship group. Nicole is also a published author. Her debut fantasy fiction novel, *Fall of the Dawn,* came out in 2023. You can find her book on Amazon.

**Billy and Kristen:** Thank you both for your wonderful insights into navigating a blended family and all you have done for the Church and the Kingdom of God. I am so proud to call you friends.

> Billy and Kristen are board members of their church and have served as volunteers in their community for many years. Their insights taken from walking through the struggles and joys of being parents of a blended family are much needed for so many families. Thank you for your heart to serve.

Finally, to my amazing beta-readers, thank you from the bottom of my heart! My lovely wife, Charlene Boyd, and dear friend, Jodi Beanland, worked so hard to make this resource as polished as possible. I could not have done without you!

# INTRODUCTION

*Genesis 2:18; 20b-25 NIV[1]*
*18 Then the Lord God said, "It is not good for the man to be alone; I will make him a helper suitable for him." 20b...but for Adam there was not found a helper suitable for him. 21 So the Lord God caused a deep sleep to fall upon the man, and he slept; then He took one of his ribs and closed up the flesh at that place. 22 And the Lord God fashioned into a woman the rib which He had taken from the man, and brought her to the man. 23 Then the man said, "At last this is bone of my bones, And flesh of my flesh; She shall be called 'woman,' Because she was taken out of man." 24 For this reason a man shall leave his father and his mother, and be joined to his wife; and they shall become one flesh. 25 And the man and his wife were both naked, but they were not ashamed.*

Marriage is the primary relationship that God created, and while we are to enjoy relationships with our children, parents, and friends, marriage is the one that is supposed to bring us the most fulfillment and joy throughout our lives.

So why is it so difficult to get right?

The answer is simple: God created the marriage relationship to reflect the closeness and intimacy that He wants to have with us, His Church. Paul talks about this profound mystery in Ephesians 5:31-32. Marriage is a reflection of the intimacy we get to enjoy with God. And Satan hates that. He has launched a full-scale war against the sanctity and importance of marriage—and thus the family—to ensure that God's people are not beautifully displaying this most sacred of relationships.

Marriage is not a walk in the park. It takes hard work to make a good marriage. It doesn't just happen the day you say, "I do." Getting married does not fix every problem you have in your life. Loneliness, lust, and addiction will still need to be handled. In many ways, marriage compounds those problems rather than making them magically go away. You know why? Because you've got someone else's problems to deal with now, too.

I am passionate about seeing God repair, heal, and restore marriages. I am zealous to see the people of God rise up and say enough is enough, to not allow the enemy to steal, destroy, and ultimately, try to kill their marriages.

I'm not trying to lay a heavy burden on you, but this reality has to be addressed when entering this great adventure called marriage. You *can* have a great marriage. And God wants that for you with all of His heart. Because when your marriage is healthy and thriving, it displays His glory and the kind of relationship He wants with you.

In the chapters of this book, you will find a wealth of knowledge and information. It is not something only to be consumed, but to draw active participation from you and your spouse. Over the last thirty-five years, I have counseled *literally* thousands of couples as they are either preparing to get married, working through problems, or even trying to figure out if they want to stay married. The one thing I have noticed about many married couples is this: they all eventually come to realize that what they thought marriage would be and the reality of marriage are two very different things. There is a difference between the romantic fantasies we build up in our minds and the very real responsibilities and struggles we find once we are actually in the trenches. Every couple has that moment of realization, some within a few days or weeks of their vows. Others, after a few years.

Some people seem to need just a little nudge in the right direction. Others seem to get addicted to counseling and want to commiserate about their woes rather than actually doing the hard work of healing, changing, and being fulfilled. Let me be clear: this book is meant to be a roadmap to bring lasting change and health to your marriage. This is not a magical, fix-all book. It will take effort and genuine introspection to see health blossom in your relationship with your spouse. Remember, it takes two to tango.

Throughout this resource, I want to see you equipped to take ownership of your marriage. Not all of these chapters may be relevant, depending on the season of marriage you are in. However, as you grow and things come up over time, you have a great resource to fall back on.

Don't feel compelled to rush through this book, either. There is no need to strive to accelerate the process, just for the sake of checking something off your to-do list. Take each chapter a week (or more) at a time: study, pray, really dig into the material, and see your marriage transformed.

It is my prayer that this resource is revolutionary for how you see your relationship with God and your spouse and how the Lord wants to use you to display His glory through your marriage and family. May God bless you as you embark on this journey to establishing a healthy marriage and strengthening your walk with God. I believe it will help you today and as a reference for years to come.

In His service,
—James Boyd

# PART 1
## MEETING EXPECTATIONS

*"Marriage is a lot like a bag of potpourri.
Nobody really knows for sure what's in there."*
—James Boyd

# PART 1

## MEETING EXPECTATIONS

# CHAPTER 1
## THE DEFRAUDMENT CLAUSE

Imagine for a moment that you are a professional artist. You have saved up for years and are finally able to purchase a set of very expensive oil paints and custom-made brushes. The cost for this is in the thousands. After months of waiting, you get your package in the mail. You take it inside, ready to start creating. But as you open the box, all you find is a haphazard collection of Crayons boxed in a disorderly fashion.

This is obviously not what you've saved for, yet when you reach out to the company to get a refund, you discover they are no longer in business. You've been scammed, you've been defrauded, and you can't do anything about it. You've lost thousands of dollars on something that normally costs under fifteen dollars. Unfortunately, you didn't get what you ordered, and now you're *stuck* with it.

How would you feel? What would you do?

We all get married thinking we know everything there is to know about our spouse. But when reality hits, we figure out real quick that there's a ton we *didn't know*. This isn't your fault. Nobody really knows what marriage is like until they are married, right? When the puppy-love stage is over, and you start dealing with real-world problems like finances, raising children, or buying a house, it could seem like your partner is a completely different person. The problem isn't with your spouse and who they are. The problem is with your false expectations of who you *thought* they would be, compared with who they *really* are.

When we are dating the person we are going to marry, we tend to put forward a false representation of who we are to put our best foot forward. It's only natural to want to present ourselves in the best possible light to stay attractive to our potential partner. Men, I bet most of you never picked your nose in front of your spouse before you were married. Ladies, I'm sure most of you never 'rooty-tooted' in front of your man before that ring was on your finger. But once the vows were read and the honeymoon was over, all bets were off, right? You may have thought, *'They're stuck with me now!'*

While these are humorous examples, the issues go even deeper and get more serious. Things start coming to the surface after the honeymoon phase is over, and we start getting *irritated* with the person we love so desperately. Why?

Misrepresentation.

We start saying things like, "It didn't seem like a big deal at the time. I thought they'd grow out of _____." (Fill in the blank with whatever that thing is.) It might have even been a deal-breaker (you would've considered seriously breaking off the engagement if you'd only known), but you went ahead and took the plunge anyway.

You may recognize some of these thoughts: *I thought they'd stop drinking. I thought they'd pay attention to me like they did when we were dating...I knew there was a lust and porn problem, but I thought I could fulfill them and they would change...I thought I'd be enough for them...*

This is invariably where bitterness and unforgiveness start to take their first foothold. If we don't take the time to deal with these compounding resentments, it will turn into unforgiveness, which will eventually turn to bitterness. And the root of bitterness has to be dealt with, or it will strangle any marriage, no matter how *in love* you were in the beginning. There will come that dreaded day when you say to yourself, *"I think I've fallen out of love; I don't know if I want to be married anymore."*

What is to be done when this happens to you? I say *when* and not *if*, because no matter what kind of marriage you find yourself in, there will be a moment when you have to face reality. We all go into marriage with expectations of what it is going to be like. Marriage is rarely what we expect. No one knows what marriage is going to be like until we get there. No parent is prepared to be a parent until they become a one. It's the same with marriage. No amount of chick-flicks and romantic books will prepare you for the reality of married life.

When the honeymoon phase is over, the fantasy of what we envisioned is overcome by the crushing weight of reality. You have to submit to the fact that your partner is not perfect and, as a matter of fact, neither are you. This letdown takes an immense amount of patience and grace as you begin to realign your rose-colored glasses and visions of your future with this person—*whom you picked*—and what it can look like going forward.

Coming to terms with this reality is imperative for this portion of healing in a Godly marriage. You picked them. Part of the problem with marriage is that you end up feeling the Defraudment Clause, that you ended up with something different than you bargained for. You do not want to admit that you were the one who chose this person. The absolute fact of the matter is you did pick them. Trading in their unseen issues for somebody else's unseen issues isn't going to fix your future.

**Letting Go of the Fantasy**

There are several common non-realities that have come up in marriage counseling sessions over the years. I have counseled so many couples who think that getting married will fix their issues. These can be issues such as lust. The Bible tells us, after all, that it is better to get married than to burn with passion, right? Or how about the issue of loneliness? Or wanting to be able to build a legacy with someone? To have children and a home of their own? The list goes on and on. In reality, no one person can fill the hole inside your heart. No one, imperfect person can help you overcome an addictive lust issue or correct a behavior that stems from childhood trauma. It is not only a fantasy, but it is incredibly unfair to your spouse to expect such things from them.

God is the only one who can fill a lonely heart or heal the pain and residue of abuse or trauma. God is the only one who can give you true, lasting freedom from addictive sins. And while it is true that God gave us the gift of marriage because *"it is not good for man to be alone,"* this does not mean that a husband or wife can fill a place that only God can fill.

It comes down to having our priorities straight. If God, and your relationship with Him, are not at the top of your priority list, no wonder everything else is out of whack. Our relationship with God is supposed to be where the rest of our relationships flow from. This comes out of the *overflow* of love, peace, and grace we receive from Him. Otherwise, we cannot love others, especially our spouses.

> *1 John 4:15-19 NIV[2] [emphasis added]*
> *15 Whoever confesses that Jesus is the Son of God, God remains in him, and he in God. 16 We have come to know and have believed the love which God has for us. God is love, and the one who remains in love remains in God, and God remains in him. 17 By this, love is perfected with us, so that we may have confidence in the day of judgment; because as He is, we also are in this world. 18 There is no fear in love, but perfect love drives out fear, because fear involves punishment, and the one who fears is not perfected in love. 19* **We love, because He first loved us.**

Did you get that? We can only love others because He first loved us. We can only love Him because He first loved us. Without His love, no other love can even exist. He is our perfect example. He is the plumb line by which we must measure everything within our lives.

Is it wrong to have expectations? Of course not. Is it wrong to punish your spouse because they are not fulfilling an expectation that was impossible for them to fulfill in the first place?

*Yes.*

In everything we do, we must make sure our hearts and attitudes are correct, and if they are not, then quick repentance is the only way to start the journey to change. It's not your spouse's job to change first. If you are waiting for them to be the first to make a move, you'll likely be waiting for a very long time. The only person you have control over is yourself. Start today by asking the Lord which areas of your life need to shift and change, then submit to the leading of the Holy Spirit to make those changes happen.

The Defraudment Clause, as I've come so fondly to refer to it, is the starting point for most marriage erosions and conflicts. This is the beginning of the seed the enemy plants within marriages that start the downward spiral of discontentment and division. These truths about your spouse—that you choose not to accept or refused to believe—are there. They are the things that cause wandering eyes, then cold, hard hearts, and ultimately, separations. But true hope and restoration are possible. It's going to take work, prayer and forgiveness. There must come a time when you face the facts of what you *thought* marriage would be versus what it has *become*. Then, through personal repentance, you can let the Lord recalibrate you for what the truth of your marriage is versus the fantasy you believed it would be.

# MARRIAGE ACTIVATION 1

Take a few minutes to read and answer these questions about what your expectations were before you got married. Take the day to pray about your responses and be ready to discuss them with your spouse/fiancé when you can set aside a good chunk of time to really get into the subject. In this discussion, you will both need to choose to be honest and listen to each other openly. Choose not to be offended.

**What Was Your Plan?**

1. What did you think marriage would be like?
2. Did it turn out the way you expected?
3. "I believe my spouse expected me to be…"
4. "I expected my mate to be more…"
5. If you were going to describe your marriage at

this time with only one word, what word would it be?
6. What do you do that expresses your love and appreciation toward your spouse?
7. What do you feel is the weakest area in your marriage right now?

Now, set aside some quiet time to discuss your answers to these questions with one another. This can be a great way to gain some insight into what your spouse was expecting out of marriage, and how you can reconcile these differences.

How will you show grace to your spouse after having this new insight into their expectations and desires? What are some ways you can meet these expectations in a realistic way?

**Prayer:**

Unmet expectations can cause grief or resentment that we tend to hold onto if not dealt with. Take some time to pray for each other and ask the Lord to realign your heart with your spouse and come to a middle ground in some of these areas. The following prayer can be a good starting place:

> *"Lord, we realize that we have had some unrealistic expectations about what marriage was supposed to be like. We also realize that You need to be the center of our marriage, and without You, we can do nothing. We ask you to fill us with your love, Father, and to help us show Your love to each other in everything we do. Help us to*

*lay down any of those unrealistic expectations and trade them for realistic expectations for one another. We submit humbly to your desire to see our marriage become a reflection of You. We ask you, Holy Spirit, to lead and guide our words and actions from this day forward. Give us eyes to see each other as You see the other. Give us ears to hear how You speak about them. Renew the love for one another we once had, Lord. We lay down every resentment or root of unforgiveness and bitterness before You and ask You to cleanse our hearts. In Your powerful name, Amen."*

If there are any places of unforgiveness that you have been holding against each other, take this time to confess and ask for forgiveness from the other person. *This is not meant to be a competition of who hurt who more.* Genuinely listen and then ask the Holy Spirit to help you forgive so that restoration and healing can take place.

# CHAPTER 2
## COUNT THE COST OF MARRIAGE

*Luke 14:25-33 NIV[3] [emphasis added]*
*25 Large crowds were traveling with Jesus, and turning to them he said: 26 "If anyone comes to me and does not hate father and mother, wife and children, brothers and sisters—yes, even their own life—such a person cannot be my disciple. 27 And whoever does not carry their cross and follow me cannot be my disciple. 28 "Suppose one of you wants to build a tower.* **Won't you first sit down and estimate the cost to see if you have enough money to complete it?** *29 For if you lay the foundation and are not able to finish it, everyone who sees it will ridicule you, 30 saying, 'This person began to build and wasn't able to finish.' 31 "Or suppose a king is about to go to war against another king. Won't he first sit down and consider whether he is able with ten thousand men to oppose the one coming against him with twenty thousand? 32 If he is not able, he will send a delegation while the other is still a long way off and will ask for terms of peace. 33* **In the same way, those of you who do not give up everything you have cannot be my disciples.**

The cost of being a spouse is very similar to being a disciple. Jesus was explaining in Luke 14 that in order to follow Him, we would have to give up everything. Our love for Him must be the first priority that guides our every thought and action. It is why baptism is such a powerful and necessary part of our Christian walk. It symbolizes dying to our old self, our sinful desires, and the world that we used to take part in. When we come to Him, He makes us a new creation (2 Corinthians 5:17). In the same way, when we embark on our marriage journeys, we leave behind our old, single lives and are joined with our spouse, becoming one with them. This concept is reminiscent of Ephesians 2:15, where Paul describes how, in Christ, Jews and Gentiles (those not of Jewish descent) are all brought together in unity, creating One New Person. When we are joined with our spouse, it's no longer "My stuff, your stuff", it's "our stuff". (*Singular.*) In the kingdom of God, one plus one does not equal two—it equals *one*. Paul calls this a profound mystery, also in Ephesians, speaking of Christ and the Church. In order to become this one new unit as a married couple, it is going to cost you. Just as it says in Luke 14, you count the cost before you start building something. In the same way, you need to count the cost of what marriage will require. If you are not willing to pay the price, your marriage is going to be rocky and conflicted at best.

Throughout this book, you will see several different sections from individuals whose perspectives I believe are important to share. I would like to highlight a story from my daughter-in-law to illustrate this point.

Before I got married, I thought I was in pretty good standing, spiritually speaking. I had worked hard to prepare myself to be a good wife and make sure I had my heart right before the Lord. But very quickly after getting married, I realized what a selfish person I was. I was honestly shocked. I had gone to Bible school and thought I'd worked through most of my "yuck". I thought I had learned to put others before myself. But I figured out real quick that living with someone day in and day out is a lot different than just getting to see that person after work, or going to hang out with them at their parents' house in the evenings. The other person comes with baggage, expectations, and weird ways of doing things.

Let me tell you, I never thought that I would be having an argument about which was the correct way to face the toilet paper roll, or the correct way to squeeze the toothpaste. I never thought we would be fighting over such dumb things, but it is the reality of marriage. I did not want to humble myself. That is, *my flesh* did not want to submit itself.

If you want to have an amazing marriage, this is where you are going to have to do something contrary to your nature—humble yourself. Die to yourself.

*"Marriage is like looking into a mirror. It shows you how selfish of a human being you really are." —Colton Boyd*

The reality I had to come to was how selfish I was. We all like to think of ourselves as selfless, especially before marriage, but no matter how prepared you try to be, you will find those pesky little things coming to the surface. Your spouse will inevitably point them out, whether in word or by giving you the "hairy eyeball" from across the dinner table. It's not even that they're trying to be mean, but they are a mirror. Through your treatment of them, or the words that come tumbling out of your mouth unbidden, they will show you what is really in your heart.

*Proverbs 27:17 NIV[4]*
  "As iron sharpens iron,
  so one person sharpens another."

Marriage is very much a sharpening process. It brings all the little things to the surface that you thought you took care of before marriage and makes you realize you have a lot more work to do. Living with someone will do that to you. A truth rarely spoken before a couple embarks on their marriage journey is that *it will cost them something*.

— NICOLE BOYD

---

## It Costs You Expectations And Desires

When you said your vows and became one with your spouse, you ceased to be the person you were before. Now you are one with another, just as God planned it. But it means that change will overtake your life. You no longer live in the same place you once did. You no longer eat, sleep, pay bills, or do anything the same way you did when you were single. Now, you and your spouse have the arduous job of taking two lives and making them one. You no longer get to do what you want and spend money on what you want without consulting the other person. Because you're not only making decisions for yourself anymore, you have to be willing to lay those things down so you can come together.

This is where things can get a little dicey. Your expectations may be different than your spouse's expectations or desires. Inevitably, there are two kinds of people in a marriage: a saver and a spender. Because of the natural tendency of these two opposites, there will ultimately be some major conflict.

There will have to be some sacrifices made for any marriage to be successful and joyful. What things can we hold on to, and what things should we let go of? The concept at the heart of this is compromise. It seems to be a dreaded word in a marriage, but it needn't be. This frame of mind may come from a very real fear that is perpetuated by our current culture. It is widely stated that when you marry, you will have to give up your autonomy, your wants, and your desires just to trudge along in misery. But that is not God's original design. To compromise in a healthy marriage does not mean that one spouse wins and the other loses. It does not mean that you keep score. It means that each spouse willingly yields their own desires for the other, in love, so the relationship can thrive—so that you both win.

Every relationship that we have in life will come with this concept of compromise. Marriage just comes with a whole lot more of it. There will have to be compromises made to the way *we* like to do things. This is so there is mutual fulfillment and respect for both parties. For example, when your spouse asks you this loaded question while you're planning a dinner out: "Where would you like to go to eat?" This question is being asked with the assumed understanding that they are strictly starting a conversation to tell you where *they* would like to go. You have probably found yourself in this situation before, and while it might have come up as a frustration, in the end, does it really matter where you go out to eat? As long as you get to eat, is it a hill worth dying on? This is just one part of understanding the sacrifice of your wants and desires within a marriage.

However, this can add to the resentments and frustrations in marriage as time goes on. These *little* things that seem inconsequential one day can become deep frustrations and resentments on another day. That's why we cannot ignore them and hope they will somehow fix themselves on their own. We must talk about those areas we are willing to adjust or compromise in, as well as those we feel strongly about that are not going to move or change.

## It Will Cost You Other Relationships

What is the *focus* of your marriage? If it is not the person you married, then any of the following examples will soon become major issues:

1. **Our Family** - The Bible says you must "leave and cleave," or "leave and be united" to your spouse (Genesis 2:24). This does not mean you have to cut all ties with your family. On the contrary, when you marry, you are not just marrying your spouse but the rest of their family, and vice versa. You are *growing* a family. But the opinions that certain family members may bring forward might not fit into your marriage. The way you did things in the family you grew up in may not be the way you want to do things in this new family. Genesis 2:24 is speaking of the need to redefine the priorities in your life. First comes God, then comes your spouse, then children, and then your extended family. The moral law of honoring your father and mother is not replaced when you get married. Rather, it is put into a different prioritization. You are called to honor God and your spouse first, then your parents and siblings. If this priority shift doesn't happen at some point, there will eventually be a marriage breakdown as you try to juggle loyalties and outside opinions.

2. **Our Work** - Although there is a relative expectation that income will be brought into the home, the making of that income can never

come between you and your spouse. Jealousy over who makes the bigger paycheck should not be a consideration. When you and your spouse both work, the money should become *our money*, not just *yours and mine*. Your work is not your life. Many people derive their identities from their jobs. But what happens if you are suddenly fired from your job? Do you cease to exist? No. That is why work must also change priority in your life and marriage. Your spouse did not marry you for your paycheck. If you are working all the time to provide or to prove yourself, but don't have enough time to spend with the one you love, your priorities are out of order.

3. **Our Leisure Activities** - In every marriage, there are hobbies, joys, and traditions that both individuals brought into the relationship. These can either be wonderful additions for you to enjoy together (or at least anticipate and understand about the other person), or they will be great areas of friction and division. Does this mean that when you get married, you will have to give up every hobby you enjoyed while you were single? Certainly not. However, the amount of time and money you spend on these things may change. These are things that must be discussed between the two of you as you go forward. Likely, it is the hobbies, creative expressions, and joys that your spouse engaged

in that were part of what drew you to them. Those leisure activities and hobbies are not what make up our full identity, but it is a big part of who we are. Learning to celebrate and engage each other in those hobbies is a great way to show you care and that you are invested in it with them. Once again, it must come down to your priorities.

4. **Our Old Friends** - Just because you got married doesn't mean all your old friends and acquaintances have to go. But there are surely some expectations that come with their involvement in your lives after you say, "I do" to your spouse. You will not spend as much time with your friends as you did when you were single. A large bulk of your time will be (and should be) dedicated to your spouse. When should a friendship be cut off? If you have friends who are trying to control and manipulate your marriage relationship, there are some boundaries that need to be established. If they refuse to abide by those boundaries, then this would certainly be a friendship that does not need to be fostered going forward. There are certainly many friendships that you will be able to keep, and even gain, from being with your spouse. We all need solid friendships with people we can learn from and with whom we can enjoy our time. Do not allow insecurity and jealousy to steal

> friendships from your spouse. Be sure to communicate with your spouse about time spent with friends if you feel it is a problem. Otherwise, try to cultivate friendships with your spouse's friends as well.

You can find your balance in marriage by discovering where your spouse fits in the middle of all this. If your spouse and pleasing them *first* is the focus of your family, work, leisure time, and friends, then I would say you're doing exactly what needs to be done and what God expects of you in the covenant of marriage. If any of these things are not as they should be, ask the Lord for the strength and wisdom to put them in the correct prioritization.

**It Costs You Your Autonomy**

As obvious as this may seem, so many people have a hard time when it comes to giving up their autonomy. It can be especially difficult for people who get married later on in life. They have gotten set in their ways, and when someone else comes in and tries to change how they do things, it can cause a lot of friction.

Over the years, I have counseled many couples who have chosen to get married later in life or those who have been single for many years, and they do not understand the conflicts that will arise from *my way vs. your way* of doing something. This could manifest in several ways, such as how to manage finances, gardening, house chores, or even which cupboard the coffee cups are supposed to go in. Obviously, some of these issues are more significant than the others, but if not adequately navigated, they can become a source of resentment and frustration that will separate and divide a marriage.

I once had a couple set an appointment with me for my assistance that were struggling in an impassable marital dispute. When they walked in, they sat in separate locations in my office. From the body language and distance between them, I realized this must be a very serious situation. After I opened in prayer, I asked them what I could do to assist them in helping resolve their frustration with one another. I was truly baffled at what happened next.

After an uncomfortably long time of them staring at me and then each other, the wife finally broke the ice and said, "Pastor, we know how busy you are, but we've had an ongoing conflict in our marriage for quite some time that we could use your assistance in correcting."

I said, "Please tell me what has caused this obvious frustration and division between you."

She said, "He refuses to rinse the dishes before he puts them in the dishwasher!"

Her husband immediately sat forward and said, "Why would I have a dishwasher if I have to touch them twice, when the dishwasher is there to *wash the dishes*?"

"Yes, but then the dishwasher bakes on all the *crusties* when you don't scrub them off first. And we have to just wash them all over again!"

He immediately turned to her and said, "Just put them back in the dishwasher!"

It was all I could do not to burst out in hysterical laughter, thinking this was some kind of joke. My board of elders had to have paid this couple to come mess with me. Once I regained my composure from all the thoughts swimming around my head and expecting at any moment someone to burst into my office and exclaim, "April fools," even though it wasn't April, I finally came to realize they were *very* serious. They had made an appointment with me to help them settle their conflict surrounding the proper way to load the dishwasher. As I sat there trying to figure out some scripture to springboard off of to give my response a more logical solution, this question came to my mind. "Are you financially stable and solid with your money?"

That seemed to take both of them back for a few moments, and finally, one of them kindly said, "Pastor, I truly don't know what that has to do with this situation, but yes, we both make great money and live very comfortable and blessed lives."

I said, "Then I've got your answer. This is going to be the shortest counseling session you've ever seen." They both leaned forward to receive my next great piece of advice. I calmly offered the solution, "Why don't you both just buy separate dishwashers? Then you can each load them however you want, and you won't ever have this frustration again."

Obviously, buying two dishwashers was unfeasible, but they burst out laughing and soon came to a resolution they both felt comfortable with. The husband agreed to rinse the dishes before putting them in the dishwasher, and the wife agreed not to micro-manage how the dishes were loaded.

Why do we allow the smallest, most insignificant things to steal our joy and happiness within our marriage? The simplest answer is, again, selfishness. When we were dating our spouse, we would have bent over backward to serve them, just to see a smile on their face. But after a few years of marriage, we settle into our new lives, and we no longer want the inconvenience of adding an extra step. Tiredness, busyness, and downright laziness come in, and we start to take the one we love for granted.

In the above dishwasher example, would it really have been that difficult for the husband to spend an extra thirty seconds washing each dish to make sure they came out clean and sparkling for his wife? No. Would it have killed the wife to not be OCD about how the dishes were stacked in the dishwasher? No. Comfort breeds contempt. We get comfortable and set in our ways, and we stop thinking about the other person first.

Setting aside our autonomy means adjusting to the needs of our spouses, even if it's something we don't agree with, or causing inconvenience in adding an extra step to make them happy. Think of a situation in your life with your spouse, something that is small but drives you crazy. Is it really worth sacrificing your marriage for?

## It Costs You Your Dreams

Maybe the most difficult thing to lay down is your dreams. It can feel like something is dying when you lay down a personal dream and wonder if you will ever get it back. Your life is not your own anymore. You are now building it with another person, and that can be a very scary reality to humble yourself to. But this is necessary if you want to enjoy all the blessings that marriage has to offer. You will make these sacrifices, not because your dreams don't matter, but because marriage is about creating something bigger than yourselves. When you choose to lay something down for your spouse, you're saying, "Our relationship matters more than my individual preference." That kind of humility and love builds trust, and over time, it deepens the bond in a way that chasing separate dreams never could.

As we dive deeper into in the next section, I want to stress that if we do not have a proper relationship with Jesus and operate in His defining characteristic, then we cannot come to marriage with the proper perspective. Jesus' defining characteristic in His life and ministry, and the only one he defined himself with, is to be a servant. Servanthood means putting the other person first and above ourselves in everything. This is when dreams come true—and allows us to fulfill our purpose and destiny in Christ.

## Repentance Restores the Standard

The single most powerful tool when it comes to overcoming selfishness is repentance. How have you been selfish with your spouse? You can probably pinpoint at least one, if not several, areas. But it doesn't mean you have to stay stuck there. Repentance is the key to combating selfishness and to restoring the standard of how God created a loving, healthy marriage to operate. Repentance means to turn from sin, but not only that, it means to change the way you think. Being sorry for selfish behavior is not enough. Repentance requires action. For example, taking out the trash is a perfect scenario. Perhaps this is your husband's job on a normal day. But what if one day, he has just come home from a twelve-hour shift and just wants to shower and change, and relax for a bit? Are you going to be mad when he doesn't see that the trash is overflowing and immediately take it out? Instead, maybe you could take it out for him this time, without saying a word, and serve him in this area? Is it really that difficult to take two minutes and take out the trash? No. Repentance takes humility. No one wants to lower themselves and take out the garbage. No one wants to pause their video game to go clean something. Especially when it's not their job. When you turn from what is your norm and start doing things to serve your spouse, this is true repentance.

What is the standard that we're supposed to be shooting for? Unfortunately, we're not living in a perfect, Garden of Eden kind of world. We live in a fallen world, where no one is perfect, and thus our marriages are going to constantly face bombardment from the enemy. Again, Satan hates it when people actually display what God originally intended for healthy marriages. What does it take to combat that selfishness, which is so easy to slip into? Servanthood. Jesus displayed this so beautifully on the night he was arrested.

> *John 13:1-17 NIV[5] [emphasis added]*
> *1 It was just before the Passover Festival. Jesus knew that the hour had come for him to leave this world and go to the Father. Having loved his own who were in the world, he loved them to the end. 2 The evening meal was in progress, and the devil had already prompted Judas, the son of Simon Iscariot, to betray Jesus. 3 Jesus knew that the Father had put all things under his power, and*

*that he had come from God and was returning to God; 4 so he got up from the meal, took off his outer clothing, and wrapped a towel around his waist. 5 After that, he poured water into a basin and began to wash his disciples' feet, drying them with the towel that was wrapped around him. 6 He came to Simon Peter, who said to him, "Lord, are you going to wash my feet?" 7 Jesus replied, "You do not realize now what I am doing, but later you will understand." 8 "No," said Peter, "you shall never wash my feet." Jesus answered, "Unless I wash you, you have no part with me." 9 "Then, Lord," Simon Peter replied, "not just my feet but my hands and my head as well!" 10 Jesus answered, "Those who have had a bath need only to wash their feet; their whole body is clean. And you are clean, though not every one of you." 11 For he knew who was going to betray him, and that was why he said not every one was clean. 12 When he had finished washing their feet, he put on his clothes and returned to his place. "Do you understand what I have done for you?" he asked them. 13 "You call me 'Teacher' and 'Lord,' and rightly so, for that is what I am.* **14 Now that I, your Lord and Teacher, have washed your feet, you also should wash one another's feet.** *15 I have set you an example that you should do as I have done for you. 16 Very truly I tell you, no servant is greater than his master, nor is a messenger greater than the one who sent him.* **17 Now that you know these things, you will be blessed if you do them.**

We all want to have a blessed marriage, right? Of course, we do. The question is, are you willing to lay down your wants, your desires, and your life in order to serve your spouse? Husbands, when she's been up every two hours feeding your newborn, are you willing to get up and change the baby's diaper so she can get some sleep? Wives, are you willing to get up a little earlier and make him a scrumptious lunch before he heads off to work a twelve-hour shift? I don't care if society says it's degrading for a wife to go make their man a sandwich. We do not live by the constructs of our modern age, feminism, or any other kind of "ism" that is pervading our culture.

We are called to live *above* the culture. This world is not our home. We are just passing through. If we want to kill selfishness and pave the way for a marriage that can truly thrive, our marriages must align with God's Word. They are going to look different than the worldly marriages around us.

> *2 Corinthians 5:14-21 NIV[6] [emphasis added]*
> *14 For Christ's love compels us, because we are convinced that one died for all, and therefore all died.* ***15 And he died for all, that those who live should no longer live for themselves but for him who died for them and was raised again.*** *16 So from now on we regard no one from a worldly point of view. Though we once regarded Christ in this way, we do so no longer. 17 Therefore, if anyone is in Christ, the new creation has come: The old has gone, the new is here! 18 All this is from God, who reconciled us to himself through Christ and gave us the ministry of reconciliation: 19 that God was reconciling the world to himself in Christ, not counting people's sins against them. And he has committed to us the message*

> *of reconciliation. **20 We are therefore Christ's ambassadors**, as though God were making his appeal through us. We implore you on Christ's behalf: Be reconciled to God. **21** God made him who had no sin to be sin for us, so that in him we might become the righteousness of God.*

## Repentance Response

The assumption has been made throughout the reading of this book that both parties have asked Jesus Christ to be Lord of their life. Because that assumption was made, we need to make sure that it is a discussion piece before we go any further in the book. If both, *not just one*, of the parties in a marriage are not serving God with all their heart, mind, and soul, the possibility of that marriage being godly is very slim.

If you have a spouse who is not serving God, 1 Corinthians 7 talks about how to cover and respond to an unbelieving spouse:

> *1 Corinthians 7:12-16 NIV[7]*
> *12 To the rest I say this (I, not the Lord): If any brother has a wife who is not a believer and she is willing to live with him, he must not divorce her. 13 And if a woman has a husband who is not a believer and he is willing to live with her, she must not divorce him. 14 For the unbelieving husband has been sanctified through his wife, and the unbelieving wife has been sanctified through her believing husband. Otherwise your children would be unclean, but as it is, they are*

*holy.* **15** *But if the unbeliever leaves, let it be so. The brother or the sister is not bound in such circumstances; God has called us to live in peace.* **16** *How do you know, wife, whether you will save your husband? Or, how do you know, husband, whether you will save your wife?*

The one who has not surrendered their life to Christ will always come from a biased and selfish perspective, because they do not understand why Jesus came and that His sole purpose was to be a servant and die for our sins. In marriage, if your sole purpose isn't to be a servant and to repent to one another for your faults, then you're never going to have a godly and healthy marriage. Before we go any further in this information, if one or both of you have never received Christ, that needs to take place immediately.

Pray this out loud together as a couple:

*Dear Jesus, we ask You right this moment to become the Lord of our lives. We believe that You came to be a servant to all and to give Your life for our sins. I ask for You to forgive me of all of the selfishness that I have partnered with in my life, for all those things that have separated me from Your favor and love. It is my desire to follow Your example and to be a servant in all areas of my life, especially in my marriage. Thank You, Lord, for forgiving me, and from this day forward, I will surrender all of me and serve You and others. Amen.*

Now that you have surrendered your lives to Jesus

Christ, we can understand what this next question truly means. What is an ambassador?

An ambassador does not act on their own will, but represents the will of their country of origin. In the same way, when we accept Christ as our Lord and Savior, we are no longer acting on our own whims and selfish desires. That is what it means to *live above the culture.* Christ lives through us. We no longer bow to the winds of the ever-shifting cultural norms, but to the mandates set before us in scripture. Where the world says, "I will when they do…" We say, "I have pledged my life to serve you, no matter if you do anything for me in return." Where the world says, "My way or the highway…" We say, "His will be done, not mine." Jesus did not follow His own desires and wants when He went to the cross. In fact, He asked God the Father to let the cup of suffering pass from Him twice before He submitted to the most excruciating and humiliating death imaginable. In the Garden of Gethsemane, when He was praying for His disciples and you and me, He said, *"not my will, but yours be done."* (Luke 22:42).

How much more should we die to our own selfishness for the sake of the person we claim to love?

Ask yourself, do you really love your spouse? If so, then you would be willing to lay down your life for them. Do you really honor them? Then you should put aside your own wants to serve them. Jesus counted the cost before He went to the cross. He looked through the annals of time when He was praying in that Garden. He saw you and said, "They're worth it." That should bring tears to our eyes and conviction to our hearts. We are called to live as laid-down lovers of the Most High God. If Jesus gave everything for us on the cross so we could be reunited and restored to the Father, then we can certainly ask for His help and empowerment to show that same kind of love to our spouse.

Let me assure you—you cannot do this out of your own strength or power. We each need His help to lay down our selfishness. But that is the beauty of it: He is willing and able to lead and guide us as we count the cost and submit to His will as we love our spouses. This is not only probable, it is made possible by the blood that Jesus shed for us. Isn't it good news that He doesn't expect us to walk this out alone?

> *Philippians 1:3-6 NIV[8] [emphasis added]*
> *3 I thank my God every time I remember you. 4 In all my prayers for all of you, I always pray with joy 5 because of your partnership in the gospel from the first day until now,* ***6 being confident of this, that he who began a good work in you will carry it on to completion until the day of Christ Jesus.***

He began the good work in you. He was there on the day of your marriage, and He said a hearty, "Amen!" If you will lovingly submit to Him, He is faithful to complete the good work in you. As long as you have breath in your lungs, you can become a better spouse, displaying His love and kindness in everything you do. Step out today, and see what God will do.

## MARRIAGE ACTIVATION 2

If you said the prayer for repentance, spend a few moments discussing how that has made you feel and the next steps that you should take going forward. I strongly encourage you to get involved in a local church. You may also reach out to us here at Refuge City Church via the following:

- Church Office: 541-882-1668
- Church Website: http://refugecity.church

Marriage will cost you your autonomy, your identity, and even your wants and desires. Because it's not all about you. This activation is all about finding the root cause of conflict that may be fueled by selfishness.

1. Separately from your spouse, take some time to really think about some areas of selfishness in your life that may be creating conflict in your

relationship. Write those areas down for discussion.
2. Pray throughout the day for God to help you in these areas, and think about how your actions may be affecting your spouse. Take a walk in their shoes. Then think of one way you can lay down your selfishness and think of your spouse first.
3. The only person you can change is you. If there are areas that you have been selfish and need to repent of, do so with your spouse now.

Afterward, take some time to pray this with each other:

*"Lord, I realize that I have been selfish in _____. Please forgive me and help me to see my spouse as you see them. Help me to lay aside my way and think of them first. I want to be the wife/husband that You created me to be. In Jesus name, Amen."*

# CHAPTER 3

## IF MARRIAGE WAS AN ISLAND

Have you ever wondered what it would be like to be stranded on a deserted island with your spouse? You would no longer have to worry about money, jobs, your commute, or even keeping up with the house. On this island, you have everything you need as far as food, and you have more than enough raw material to build a shelter. How would your attitude change toward your spouse with this perspective in mind?

It sounds like paradise for some and a nightmare for others. But why? Why would being stranded with your spouse be so terrible? I can tell you, it's most likely not the other person. While they may have some quirks that drive you crazy at times, it is most likely outside influences that have put a strain on your relationship and marriage.

We have outside influences coming at us from every direction. There is a constant noise of family opinions, friendships that must be maintained, co-workers and their demands, and constant distractions from movies, books, and social media telling us how our marriage should be and what needs to be fixed to make it perfect.

The list goes on and on. What if you had none of these outside influences? What if you could take a breath and have nothing to worry about, except what needed to be done next to survive? All that you were responsible for was your survival and taking care of one another. How would your attitude and stress level change? How much better would you know your spouse than you do now? How much closer would you be with them?

I have asked couples this question in counseling sessions many times. I remember one session in particular:

This couple had been married for only a few years, and they were already dealing with regrets and Defraudment Clause conflicts. As we started talking, it became very clear, very fast, that they had a third person who was influencing almost every area of their lives and home. This person was highly valued and important to the wife. However, this person was the complete opposite for the husband, causing no end of strife and frustration for him. This third-party contributor had been the wife's best friend since childhood. The best friend was a very alpha-dominant person who had basically controlled the life of this wife before she met her husband. She was the secret whisperer into this wife's ear concerning everything that her husband did, said, and how they lived. If this best friend didn't like something concerning the husband, the wife was immediately scolded, manipulated, and controlled until things went the way of this friend.

This was an ongoing battle that had a relatively simple answer. Thus, the reason I decided to use the marriage-is-like-an-island scenario during their session. I asked this couple how they thought their marriage would be currently if they were stranded on a deserted island and this third-party individual was nowhere to be found. Instantly, the whole demographic of the counseling session changed. The man leaned forward and began to ask questions about this scenario and how he could provide, care for, and love his spouse with the best resources they had available. The wife, soon after, began stating a list of her contributions for their survival and how they would make it through no matter what. Soon, they were planning their life together on the island, and they were describing every detail. The wife even suggested that they could revert to Genesis 2:25 and how it was in the Garden of Eden (*they were both naked and unashamed*). Then they both held hands and started giggling.

    The husband then suggested something else they could implement on their island, and that's when it happened. The wife abruptly stopped playing with the storyline and said, "We can't do that because Third Party Influencer wouldn't like it." At this point in the counseling session, everything came to a standstill. They instantly realized the problem and to whom their problems were attributed. It wasn't with their marriage, their love, or their relationship —it was the Third Party Influencer having way too much involvement in their lives and future. It was at this point that the session got overwhelmingly direct and specific. It was time for the wife to lay down new ground rules and parameters with her friend over her involvement in their marriage. A plan was discussed and followed through with.

    Soon after, the best friend told the wife she did not feel

comfortable with the new arrangement and that they could no longer be best friends. This was the best thing that ever happened to this marriage. Later, this so-called friend found another couple to manipulate and torment, and the last that I'd heard, they were in the process of getting a divorce.

Here's the moral to this story: *if you treat your marriage like an island*, nothing and no one can come between you.

# MARRIAGE ACTIVATION 3

Eradicating outside voices and distractions is a must when coming together with your spouse. No one can tell you how best to conduct your marriage relationship, outside of the Holy Spirit. Throughout these exercises, think of how distractions may be stealing some of the joy and peace from your relationship.

1. Imagine for a moment what it would be like to be stranded on a deserted island with your spouse. How would your priorities change? What are the things (if any) that you would fight over?
2. Now, think about where you are today. What are some outside influences that are stealing from your joy or putting stress on your relationship with your spouse? How can you fix those immediately?

3. We cannot drown out and ignore the world we live in. But how long has it been since you and your spouse had some time to yourselves? How long has it been since you went on a date, turned off your cellphones, and just talked?

**This is your assignment:**

Take your spouse out on a date. *Before you move on to the next chapter,* you are to find a sitter for the kids, and take one evening to put away all distractions and spend quality time together. This is not for discussing bills or events on the calendar. Take time to get to know each other again, apart from a business-meeting style date. Here are some questions you can ask each other:

- What are you most looking forward to this year?
- What is a dream that God has been placing on your heart lately (that I may or may not know about)? How are you feeling about that dream? How can I come alongside you to see that become a reality?
- What is your favorite memory of our life together so far?
- What is a time you have laughed until your ribs hurt? (Could be something you've experienced together or separately.)
- What has God been speaking to you lately in your Bible study and prayer time?
- Where do you see our marriage in five years?

- What is something you've always wanted to do but haven't gotten around to yet?
- When was the moment you first knew you were in love with me?

# CHAPTER 4

## MY JOB, YOUR JOB

There was a time when my wife and I had young adults over to our house every week and spent time building relationships and discipling. We had been married for approximately 12 years at the time, and we had worked many of those first-year hiccups out of our marriage. My wife was a stay-at-home mom and would spend her days taking care of the home, cooking, cleaning, and taking care of the kids when they got home from school.

We had developed a routine that when I came home from the church, she would come out of whatever room she was in, kiss me, and bring me a glass of tea and the remote control to the TV. On one of these days we had a young lady who was a part of our young adults discipleship group over to the house. We had become good friends with her over the years, and she was helping my wife cook dinner on this specific evening, and just to relax with us. I came into the house as usual, changed out of my work clothes, and sat down in my chair. However, my wife did not come and kiss me or give me any tea or the remote.

My wife and this young woman were talking in the kitchen, having a wonderful time. I spoke up, asking where the remote and my glass of tea were. Before my wife was able to answer, the young lady piped up and said, "Get it yourself. Your legs aren't broken, are they?"

I thought my wife's eyeballs were going to pop out of her head. Without a word to me, she motioned this young lady to follow her into the other room. I proceeded to get up and find the remote, and turn on a hunting show while the ladies were having a come-to-Jesus-moment. Afterward, the young lady came out with my wife and promptly came over to me to apologize. She was very sweet, and of course, all was forgiven. My wife had explained to her that this was the way we conducted our marriage. It wasn't that I couldn't get myself a glass of tea or find the remote. It was that my wife wanted to serve me, especially after having a long day at the office.

When we got married, she had said that she wanted to be a stay-at-home wife and mother. Her ministry wasn't to the church; it was to me and our family.

You see, we all have these preconceived notions of what should or should not be in a marriage. And as much as we wouldn't want to admit it, we have expectations of what each partner will do. Cleaning the garage and mowing the lawn? That's *men's work*. Cooking, cleaning, and taking care of the home? That's *women's work*.

However, it may not be the same throughout every

marriage. I knew a young couple where the wife loved mowing the lawn. It was actually her favorite pastime, being out in the sunshine and getting an hour or two to herself to think and re-energize. It made her whole week. Her husband was more than happy to give her that job because his allergies made it a living nightmare to contend with the yard. As luck would have it, the husband didn't mind doing the dishes. So they switched roles. Which worked great for their relationship. The point is not to allow outside influences to make you feel guilty about how you set up your marriage roles, your life, and your home.

Another example of this in my own marriage, and quite a comical one, was when my wife had been sick for several days. There were dishes piled everywhere when I came home from the church. My wife had just filled the sink with water to start doing the mountain of dishes. Instead of going to change and sit in my chair, I decided to help her out. Instead of getting a "thank-you", I got an immediate scolding from my wife. "Why do I always have to do the dishes? You know what, I am going to go mow the lawn, and you can stay here and deal with the mess in this kitchen."

I was fairly blindsided by her intensity, but I agreed that we could trade. She changed her clothes, and I took her out to show her how to get the push mower started. However, I told her that I would only get it started for her once, and then she would be on her own. She agreed to this and started mowing, while I went back inside and began doing the dishes and cleaning the kitchen.

After a little while, I heard the rumble of the mower go

quiet. I had told her she would have to empty the bag a couple of times. I assumed she was going to empty it, and then I'd hear the mower turn back on. I soon heard her pulling the crank, but the mower would not turn over. I expected her to come back in and ask for help, but she did not appear. For half an hour, she wrestled with the mower to no avail. I finished the dishes by this time and had gone to sit down in my chair.

Finally, my wife came back in, her hands raised. "Alright, you win. I don't want to trade jobs. I will never complain about the dishes if you just take back the mowing!" It has been a great story and laugh from that moment on. More importantly, we both settled into our roles without resentment and contention.

**Take a Walk in Each Other's Shoes**

A marriage, especially a Christian one, is supposed to be a thing of intense beauty, love, and joy. It is a reflection of Jesus as the Groom, and the Church as the Bride. However, too often, this is just not the case. Sadly, many marriages, even those where both partners are believers, are in serious turmoil. You know the story: a couple is deeply in love—when you see one, you see the other. They do everything together, they talk about their futures, and show their love for one another in a million little, seemingly insignificant ways. They date like this for several months or even years. Finally, they reach a point where they feel that they just can't bear to be apart any longer, and they get married. For a while, they are wonderfully happy. Then, after the dust settles and they get used to being together, it seems that the old flame that burned so brightly is now just a smoldering ember. Where before she never had to open a door, now she opens them all. Where before he never saw her unless she was looking her best, now, all he seems to see is her at her worst. There are issues that come up now that find them acting like warring nations instead of one flesh united in love.

Most married folks will know exactly what I am talking about. When things reach this point, many couples throw in the towel and begin to look for fulfillment in someone else, and then eventually they transition to divorce court. If they do not choose this route, they may decide to stay together for the children's sake. Either way, there is division where God intended for there to be harmony. How and why do things reach this point? They either lack the tools they need to keep their home together, or they lack the commitment that is necessary to make changes to see healing and hope. I am convinced, however, that things do not have to end that way.

Is there hope for a marriage that seems to have gone sour? Is there a way to rekindle the old flame? Yes! But don't look for magic formulas. Don't expect sudden breakthroughs that change everything radically and permanently. If you're going to turn *dreadlock* into *wedlock*, you are going to have to work at it. It will require effort, humility, a deep commitment to the relationship, and above all, a willingness to do everything God's way.

There are certain guidelines laid out in the Bible that, if followed, will make a difference in our marriages immediately.

### 1. Don't Make Your Choices or Decisions Based on a Wrong Value System

We all have to make choices in life. We have to make choices about relationships, purchases, careers, ministries, education, volunteering, and entertainment.

The values that guide these choices will, in large part, determine whether these choices result in a blessed life or a messed-up life. Making decisions based on wrong values is one way to quickly make a mess of your marriage.

I could give many examples of wrong values, but the list would certainly include sensuality, materialism, selfishness, unresolved conflict, and godlessness.

In other words, we should not make our decisions based on what is pleasing to our senses (sensuality). Our choices should not be based on what will generate the most income or enable us to gain the most possessions. We should not make our decisions on purely selfish motives, which means considering what we want but not what God wants. We have to make our decisions based on God's word and His instructions. God's word is the greatest guidebook for marriage and relationships that has ever been written. Read it and use it!

### 2. Be Certain of Your Salvation

It is imperative that both partners in the marriage covenant be believers in Jesus and strive to continually serve God above all. An unequal yoke produces a relationship that is totally out of balance. In 2 Corinthians 6:14, Paul warns against being unequally yoked with unbelievers. The imagery we get from this passage comes from a time where carts were pulled by pairs of oxen connected by a yoke. A yoke was a wooden contraption that would rest on the oxen's necks, fastening the two animals together. This yoke allowed them to pull the weight of the cart in unison. It also served to distribute the weight of the cart so the oxen could pull it more efficiently, and carry more weight between the two of them versus one.

If one ox was much weaker than the other, the stronger one would drag it along and injure the weaker. Paul uses this illustration to show that we should not be yoked with unbelievers, because that will cause an imbalance in the relationship. Another way to say this is to think of standing on a box. The Christian is one who is represented by standing on a box, and an unbeliever on the ground. It is much easier to pull someone down than it is to pull someone up. The influence of the unbeliever will lead the believer astray, pulling them down. Without the presence of Christ dwelling in both hearts, the marriage is doomed to trouble from the start. However, in a home where both spouses are saved and striving to serve the Lord, the Holy Spirit can equip them to handle their difficulties, differences, and problems. When you are both pulling the yoke in the same direction, with the same goal in mind, it is much easier to live for the Lord.

There are definite cases where a believer and a nonbeliever have a good marriage, but they are the exception and not the rule. Just because your spouse comes to church once a month doesn't mean they are saved and have a relationship with Christ. More often than not, the unbeliever will drag the believer down to their standard of living. No

Christian home will be successful without an ever-deepening relationship with God on the part of both spouses. I say both, because there will also be problems when one is seeking after the Lord and the other is at a standstill in their Christian walk. There will be a different set of family goals and priorities when Jesus isn't the focus of both lives. Everything rises or falls on your relationship with God. Don't have the attitude that you can change them. First, if you love someone, you shouldn't want to change them. Second, God—not you— is in control of salvation and change.

What do you do if you're stuck?

As was stated, also in Chapter 2, the following is the biblical perspective on staying with a spouse after you've received Christ, and they are still not a Christian. 1 Corinthians 7 was very clear on this, that you are to stay married to them, as long as they are totally in agreement with your love and walk with Christ being first in your life. If they are, then your salvation and example at some point will cover them, which will lead them to Christ over time. If they do not want you to continue to be a Christian, because it has changed your lifestyle and marriage relationship too drastically, then according to 1 Corinthians 7, Jesus comes first. So, you will have to choose Him over staying with your spouse.

There are several action steps you can take if you find yourself in this situation. First, pray faithfully for your spouse and model Christ's love in everything you do. It is by observing your love for Jesus and others that you will have the opportunity to introduce your spouse to the Lord. Second, you must set healthy boundaries and stay connected to a Christian community. You cannot grow in your Christian walk alone. Having strong believers by your side to encourage and help you along the way is imperative. Finally, you must wait on the Holy Spirit's timing. Persevere to see your spouse come to know Jesus as their Lord and Savior—not just for you, but for them.

3. **Sharpen and Serve Each Other.**

A marriage can't work unless you're willing to sharpen each other: physically, spiritually, and emotionally. Help one another become better people. Colossians 4:6 goes a long way in doing that. It says, *"Let your speech be always with grace, seasoned with salt, that you may know how to answer everyone."*

Watch your words. They will either build up or tear down your spouse. Your words have power. Proverbs 18:21 says, *"Death and life are in the power of the tongue; those who love it will eat its fruit."* Are you building your spouse up with words of life, or bringing destruction to their hearts with criticism and complaints? It is said that for every negative word spoken, it takes five positive ones to cancel it out. Your partner has an emotional bank account; it takes five positive deposits for every negative withdrawal. What are you putting in?

Does this mean that you don't need to communicate hard truths at times? No. But the Word of God says to speak the truth *in love*. There may be times when you need to point out a flaw to your spouse. This is not so you can feel vindicated, but so that they have the opportunity to see it and submit to the Holy Spirit to help bring the change that is needed. The same goes vice versa. When you lovingly submit to one another, God can use you to sharpen one another. In other words, God uses you to help each other grow. Dull knives cause more damage than sharp ones. In the same way, flippant, angry, sarcastic words can stick with your spouse for longer than we count on, and continue to wreak havoc for years to come. You must use positive, encouraging words to build up and edify each other.

Here is an example. A young couple was once going through a difficult season, especially the husband, with his desire and longing to work in the church. He had been working as a volunteer for some time, and he felt he was in line for an opportunity to be on staff in a full-time salaried position. He was constantly complaining about this to his wife. This husband had often said, "I deserve a real position. It should be mine by now. I could do a much better job." At one point, they were driving in the car, and the husband was again complaining about his lack of recognition and the promotion to become the pastor like he wanted. He said, "I just want my chance to be the pastor God wants me to be. It feels like this guy (another pastor on staff) is in my house leading something that belongs to me." The wife was very quiet and felt like God was speaking something very simple but profound to her. She responded quietly, "It's not your house. It's God's house." Her husband got very quiet for a long time and finally said, "You are right." He had been trying to earn promotion in his own power, instead of waiting for God's timing. If we humble ourselves, God's word says He will lift us up (Luke 14:11).

This is just one example where someone's words were

filled with grace, even if the other person didn't like what was being said in the moment. It sharpened them both and opened his eyes to what was causing the conflict and ultimately the lack of promotion from the Lord to come his way.

# MARRIAGE ACTIVATION 4

The Word tells us that we should treat others as we would want to be treated. Take some time to take a walk in your spouse's shoes, and purpose to appreciate and praise them for all they do.

1. During the next week, switch chores.

- If you've never done the dishes, it's your turn.
- If you've never mowed the lawn/shoveled snow off the walk/pulled weeds out of the flower beds, it's your turn.
- If you've never vacuumed, it's your turn.
- If you've never cooked an entire meal, it's your turn.
- If you've never changed the oil in the car or had to take the car to the mechanic, it's your turn.
- If you've never done all of the laundry, it's your turn.

*\*Do not move forward until you have done the above exercise for the allotted one-week period.*

2. Great job! How did switching roles affect you? Did you resent any of the roles? Did it give you a greater appreciation for what the other person does? Take some time to discuss how you felt while fulfilling the other's role, and express appreciation for what they do that you may have taken for granted.
3. Now, fill a wash basin or some kind of container, and I want you each to wash each other's feet. What a perfect way to end this week with an exclamation point of renewing your vow to serve the other. As you wash their feet, tell them how much they mean to you and how you appreciate them. Then pray a prayer of servanthood over your spouse. Ask God to help you be a better servant in your marriage to your partner.

# CHAPTER 5
## MARRIAGE TUNE-UP

You've saved for years, and you finally have what you need to buy that dream car you've always wanted. You've had pictures of it hanging on your wall since you were sixteen—that '67 Mustang GT with the shiny candy apple red paint job plus all the bells and whistles you could think of. It's finally yours.

What would happen if you bought the car and never changed the oil? Or the air filter? Or the spark plugs? What would happen if you drove the car for months and years and never added coolant or other fluids? All my car people are cringing right now, aren't you? Here's the reality: this '67 Mustang beauty would not be in good working order for very long if you failed to do maintenance on the engine to keep everything running smoothly.

It is the same with your marriage.

What happens when you ignore your relationship and keep driving the car (your marriage) without taking precious time to care and maintain the important things within your relationship? There is going to come a point where you will have a breakdown and coast to the side of the road in your marriage. What are the things you have buried in your hearts? What current resentments and places of bitterness are you holding onto that are starting to overheat and cause your marriage engine to seize up? Could all this make your love for one another sputter and die?

There once was a man who had been married for quite some time, but it was obvious that his wife was disconnected and just going through the motions. On one occasion, I got an opportunity to ask her why she seemed so disconnected from her marriage. This is what she said, "My husband has bragged and bragged for years about a quote he made to me on our wedding day. He said, "I just want you to know that I love you, and if that ever changes, I'll let you know."

She continued, "I thought for the first few years or so that it was just a joke, as I did many things to try and get him to say those special words. Over the years he has told that story to lots of people, even strangers, like it was some kind of trophy to brag about. But, through it all, he has kept to what he said that first day, and I've never been able to get him to tell me he loves me since our wedding day. It's not something I believe is worth getting a divorce over, but I have cried myself to sleep just wishing I could hear him say it one more time."

Wow! I was totally blown away when I heard this! This was a marriage that could have definitely used some maintenance. This husband totally misunderstood what it takes to maintain a healthy marriage. You cannot just say "I love you" once and expect to have intimacy with your spouse, just as you cannot change the oil in an engine only once and expect your car to function on an ongoing basis as it should. Years of frustration and questions over one arrogant statement had caused a breakdown in communication and intimacy in this marriage.

What are healthy ways to acknowledge and communicate that the filter is clogged, the oil needs changing, or a tune-up is needed? Changing these things takes humility, work, and sometimes it takes a special mechanic (counselor, pastor, or mentor). You're going to have to embrace some hard truths in order to see these changes happen. When you're preparing to go on a long road trip, you set appointments and make plans to have every part of the vehicle taken care of before leaving, so you don't break down or become stranded. Have you practiced that for your life journey with one another in marriage? Do you set aside specific times, set appointments, and make plans to maintain and be consistent in being the best for each other in your marriage? The alternative is seizing the engine of your marriage and having to start all over with a fresh rebuild. Most people just go buy a different car, rather than putting in the time to fix the old one they already have. This usually ends in a lot more pain, grief, and disappointment than they ever realized.

## What Happens When Divorce Enters the Equation?

I've observed that many people, following a divorce, will meet someone they are attracted to, and they will put forth an enormous effort to present themselves as an ideal mate to their new heartthrob. It strikes me each time, if they are thinking about divorce, why not try that same strategy with their current heartthrob—their *spouse*?

After all, think of the history you have together, which is probably not all bad. Consider how much better it would be to stay together as opposed to divorcing. Think about how much easier it could be if you tried this approach and it worked with the things you've been neglecting under the hood of your current marriage. There are some very good reasons to give this option a chance before you throw in the towel and go get the newest and latest model.

So, this is what we are diving into for this chapter: how is it possible for you as a married couple to take specific actions, right now, that could wind up blessing and restoring your marriage with just a little bit of maintenance?

I need to give you some hard truths about the situation you are in. Unless you embrace these truths, you will never be able to do what it takes to restore your marriage and make it as healthy and wonderful as it can be.

Let's start with the husbands:

## Hard Truth No. 1. LACK OF SPIRITUAL DIRECTION

If your wife is distant or seems despondent with you, it is almost certain that you have established a pattern of behavior that has caused her to want to put distance between the two of you.

Consider that this is a woman who, at one time, wanted to be close to you. She was warm. Her heart was open to you. Otherwise, she could have never married you or been intimate with you.

I say that because women are naturally emotional responders. They will respond to the emotional climate in which they find themselves. If it's a good climate, they will stay open and vulnerable. If it is not, they will shut down and close off. Most men aren't like that. So, if your wife has closed down and backed away, the only logical conclusion is that something has happened to the emotional climate to cause her to behave in a different way than when you started the engine of your marriage.

Well, guess who tends to create the emotional environment for your wife? It is usually not her. It's *you*. You create the emotional environment. The emotional climate of a marriage is the responsibility of the husband. That's why the Bible says:

> *Ephesians 5:28a-29a NIV*[9]
> *28 Husbands ought to love their wives as their own bodies... 29 No one ever hated his own body, but he feeds and cares for it...*

When a man feeds and cares for his body, what's he doing? He's creating the environment in which it can thrive. In the same way, the Bible says, a husband ought to do that for his wife—create an environment for her to survive and thrive.

Now, I know that some of you might be thinking, "Oh, but you don't know my wife." There are so many times when I have counseled men who have stated that they have already tried to change for their wives, only to be rejected or made fun of. Many have said that after years of marriage, their negative responses to their wife and her emotions have come from walls that have been built. This is due to her sarcasm and belittlement, or a lack of acknowledgment that they are trying. They often feel that their wife has no faith in them and still looks at them as that young, insecure boy she claimed to fall in love with so many years ago. It seems like the wife has not taken the time to evaluate all of the good things that have occurred within their spouse to try to be a better husband and man.

I have to acknowledge that there is some truth in this scenario. The maintenance comes into play here because instead of having proper communication and understanding with one another, we have caused resentment to boil over and create a huge mess, resulting in unforgiveness and grudges.

Gary Smalley wrote about this subject in his book called *If Only He Knew: A Valuable Guide to Knowing, Understanding, and Loving Your Wife.* I highly suggest getting this book for further reading, but the gist is this: If you don't like the lack of affection or wonder about the coldness in your wife, look at yourself first. Wives sometimes get a bad rap for being strong-willed, contentious, and sarcastic. In reality, they are only responding to the emotional climate set forth by their husband's walls. There are two contributors to the marriage. If your wife is responding in a way that shows she has lost affection or romantic love for you, the best place to look for a solution is to ask yourself what happened to start those reactions. Then, fix them.

If you're a husband, the emotional environment of the marriage is *your responsibility*.

## Hard Truth No. 2: DISSATISFACTION

If you are dissatisfied with her to the point of leaving or building walls to make her leave, it is likely that *you* have produced what you dislike in her.

Again, let's put male logic to work: this is a woman with whom you *were satisfied* with at one time. Otherwise, you wouldn't have married her.

Now, if you are the one responsible for tending the emotional garden of the marriage relationship and you're not satisfied—if the garden is full of weeds and the plants are sickly—whose fault is it? *Most likely yours.*

If you're dissatisfied with your wife, you are helping to produce what you dislike. Women are built to take what a man gives them and multiply it. For example, give a woman a *house* and she multiplies it and turns it into a *home*. Give a woman a *seed* and she will multiply it and give you a *baby*. Give your wife grief, and she will multiply it and give you one nightmare of a sarcastic headache.

Unless you come face-to-face with this fact, stop playing games, stop building walls, and stop blaming her, you will make the biggest mistake of your life. Inevitably, you are building walls that keep your wife out to protect your own heart from being rejected.

## Hard Truth No. 3: HARD-HEARTEDNESS

> *Matthew 19:7-8 NIV[10] [emphasis added]*
> "If marriage is to be permanent," the Pharisees asked, "why did Moses command that a man give his wife a

> *certificate of divorce and send her away?" Jesus replied, "Moses permitted you to divorce your wives because your <u>hearts were hard.</u>"*

Jesus guarantees that hard hearts will cause separation. Unless you admit that your heart has grown hard, the characteristics that cause a woman to feel respected, heard, and open to you, won't make sense. If you refuse to see your current reality for what it is, there is no way you will ever learn to love your wife in a way that encourages her to open her heart to you like she did when she first decided to marry you. Being hard-hearted is precisely what has happened to stop your marriage from being blessed and functioning healthily.

The characteristics listed below could help to soften her heart, tear down the walls, and cause her to fall in love with you all over again.

> *1 Peter 3:7 NIV[11]*
> *Husbands...be considerate as you live with your wives, and treat them with respect...*

The key is understanding what consideration and respect look like to a woman. I'm going to give you six characteristics that describe a man who women perceive to be considerate and respectful.

    A. **Characteristic No. 1: His Response to Her is Understanding and Tender.**

I've observed that, when it comes to marriage, almost

every woman (regardless of personality type and regardless of whether she's a stay-at-home mom or a career woman) desires to be led by their husband with understanding and tenderness. These attributes are always received as a positive motivating factor that alters conflict and coldness in the relationship.

- **Be a great listener.** Instead of thinking about your response to something your wife has said or nagged you over, you must learn to truly listen to what she is trying to say. The fact that she feels she is not being heard could be the reason for the repetition and nagging. Be understanding and tender.
- **You don't have to fix everything.** Sometimes she may just be trying to communicate what she is feeling from the depths of her heart. When you listen and understand the emotions she's experiencing, she feels safe, respected, and heard. This does not always mean she needs whatever the issue or problem she's communicating about to be fixed or changed.
- **Lead her in prayer.** Start taking the initiative to lead your wife in prayer over the matter before you instinctively try and tell her what she could do to fix it or change it. You will be amazed at how looking her in the eyes and saying I want to pray with you over this before anything else, can cause all of her frustration and anxiety to wash away.

B. **Characteristic No. 2: He Knows How To Ask For Directions.**

There really is this compulsion within us as men to always know where we're going and how we're getting there, even if we've never been there before. I know this is a joke that has been a classic for decades, but we have to be honest. It is true, men tend to hate asking for directions. When it comes to a marriage, which is a place none of us have ever been before, we are going to need to ask for directions and get some assistance from others at times.

Can you imagine how ecstatic you would be if your wife asked, "Honey, how can I become a better wife?" It would be great, wouldn't it? So, if you want your wife to do this for you, first ask her how you can be a better husband. In doing so, you'll give her hope for gaining the type of marriage she's always wanted. If she sees that you are sincere, she'll become far more responsive to your needs and desires in return. We have to remember, we've never been this way before. So we both need help with the directions.

### C. Characteristic No. 3: He Knows How To Forgive Fully.

This one goes against almost everything that our society teaches men to be. After you have been verbally abusive to your wife, do you think she would appreciate it if you admitted you were wrong and expressed sorrow that you may have hurt her? What would she do if you said, "How do you put up with such a pain-in-the-neck like me, as insensitive as I am? I'm asking you now, will you please forgive me?"

Unfortunately, for most wives, this would be their response. "I'd call the cops, because I'd know there was another man in the house that was a look-a-like for my husband."

All wives love to hear their man ask if they will forgive them. Saying, "I'm sorry," usually doesn't cut it. It might just mean, *I'm sorry you're frustrated*, or *I'm sorry you're angry*, or *I'm sorry I got caught*. That's not really a desire for forgiveness. That's just a unique way of redirecting the blame so husbands don't have to take responsibility.

### D. Characteristic No. 4: He Knows How To Compliment and Praise Her Publicly.

It's no secret that praise motivates people. When a wife knows that she is pleasing to her husband, she will be more motivated to move emotionally towards him, to submit to him, and follow his leadership.

A man who really honors and loves his wife never criticizes her publicly. My experience with my wife and in watching other couples is that even when it's delivered in a joking or non-threatening manner, criticism almost always has a negative effect. No woman wants to be humiliated and have her value diminished in front of others.

### E. Characteristic No. 5: He Knows How To Always Make Her No. 1.

Making your wife number one goes beyond words of praise and must become a tangible action. If it comes down to an evening with friends or a night with your wife, she needs to know you'd choose her because there is no one else on this planet you'd rather be with. Women notice how our eyes light up and our entire personalities change as we become excited about hunting, fishing, sports, or other activities. If your wife doesn't sense that same excitement in you when you're with her, she will begin to feel she isn't as attractive to you as your other hobbies, activities, or friends.

Now, if that sounds a little confining, here's the flip side to this: when she is satisfied that she takes first place in your life, she will encourage you to do the other things you like because she's secure in your relationship.

### F. Finally, Characteristic No. 6: He Knows How To Be The Spiritual Leader.

He doesn't leave the spiritual stuff all up to his wife. There's an interesting verse in the Bible that says...

*Ephesians 5:23 NIV[9]*
*The husband is the head of the wife.*

I'm not referencing authority or control. Men need to always remain growing in their spiritual walk with God for the betterment of themselves and their families. Husbands have to choose every day to be the example in all things to their wives and children, so they can follow his Christlike example and spiritual leadership.

The husband should want to be the spiritual leader in the marriage and home. Most women intuitively sense this. When the man attempts to fulfill that spiritual leadership role in a conscientious and willing manner, the whole family will respond in a positive way.

## Now It's The Wives' Turn

Now, it's your turn, ladies. I know you're dying to know how you can become a woman that a man feels respected, honored, and cherished by.

> *I Peter 3:1-6 NIV[11]*
> *1 Wives, in the same way submit yourselves to your own husbands so that, if any of them do not believe the word, they may be won over without words by the behavior of their wives, 2 when they see the purity and reverence of your lives. 3 Your beauty should not come from outward adornment, such as elaborate hairstyles and the wearing of gold jewelry or fine clothes. 4 Rather, it should be that of your inner self, the unfading beauty of a gentle and quiet spirit, which is of great worth in God's sight. 5 For this is the way the holy women of the past who put their hope in God used to adorn themselves. They submitted themselves to their own husbands, 6 like Sarah, who obeyed Abraham and called him her lord. You are her daughters if you do what is right and do not give way to fear.*

One night, a wife found her husband standing over their baby's crib. As he stood there looking down at the sleeping child, she saw on his face a mixture of emotions: disbelief, doubt, delight, amazement, enchantment, and skepticism. With glistening eyes, she slipped her arm around her husband, touched by this unusual display of deep emotions he was experiencing. "A penny for your thoughts," she said.

"It's amazing," he replied softly. "I just don't see how anybody can build a crib like that for only $79.95!"

It goes without saying that men are different from women. We have discussed the man's role in becoming the man that a woman can love and respect in great detail. Now, what are the wife's responsibilities in this same area?

The first, and most important aspect for saving your marriage, ladies, is for you to continue to love your husbands first, and your children second. All too often, women become mothers and throw all their efforts into being the best mother they can be. But then, something subtle and deceptive happens. She forgets she has a husband, too. This is something that happens over days, weeks, and months. You don't mean to slip into forgetfulness when it comes to your husband, but it does happen.

This is how to correct this situation:

- Love Your Husband before anything or anyone: Loving your husband is a choice based on loving God first, him second, and your family and friends after that.
- Do something to honor your husband every day. (Rom 12:10)
- Devote yourself to some special time with your husband every day. (This really doesn't have to be sexual or intimate in nature). An "I Love You" text will suffice. (Rom 12:10)
- Encourage your husband every day. (Heb 3:13)
- Sympathize with him in trials and tribulations. Stop everything and prioritize him. (1 Pet 3:8)

- Don't grumble or complain before you connect and respect. (James 5:9)
- Forgive quickly and forget even more quickly. (Luke 17:3)
- Spend time together. (Heb 10:25)

**I Will, If You Will**

We have allowed the love relationship to falter into a mindset of, "I will, if you will" lifestyle. To be a wife and love your husband, involves a long-term commitment and daily sacrifice. This is a total contrast of how the modern world views the marriage relationship. The admonishment from the Lord is for wives to love their husbands, cherish their husbands, and honor their husbands. If you were to rate yourself on a scale of 1-10 (one being not at all and ten being extremely involved), how would you rate?

Wives also have characteristics that cause a man to want to engage and stay connected. Here is that list:

A. **Characteristic No. 1: She Watches Her Motives To Be A Godly Wife First.**

*I Peter 3:1-2 NIV[11]*
*1 Wives, in the same way submit yourselves to your own husbands so that, if any of them do not believe the word, they may be won over without words by the behavior of their wives, 2 when they see the purity and reverence of your lives.*

The tendency of many wives is to view their role in a

conditional way that depends on the behavior of their husbands. For example: "I'll be the kind of wife I should be, if he's the kind of husband he should be first. He's the head and the leader, right?"

Peter suggests this wise counsel to wives: You are responsible for yourself, not your husband. Whether he changes certain behaviors and heart conditions is up to the Lord, not you. You are responsible for YOU. That means using your husband as the scapegoat won't cut it with God. God is looking at this marriage from both sides of the spouses' Christlike and biblical behaviors. This is not something you can excuse before God because your husband is supposed to be the spiritual leader. God gives expectations for both husbands and wives, and they aren't conditional on the other spouse's response.

> *Ephesians 5:22-24 NIV[9] [emphasis added]*
> *22 Wives, submit to your own husbands, as to the Lord.*
> *23 For the husband is head of the wife, as also Christ is head of the church; and He is the Savior of the body. 24 Therefore, just as the church is subject to Christ, **so let the wives** be to their own husbands in everything.*

I want to touch on the flip side of something we discussed with the husbands in the previous section. He is the spiritual leader of the household. I cannot tell you how many times I have counseled couples where the wife has prayed for her husband to become the spiritual leader of the house. But there is an insecurity that creeps up when he actually takes the lead and starts doing it. You cannot pray that your husband becomes the spiritual leader, and then be offended that he took your job. Many women have taken the lead in praying over their children, reading the Word with them, and leading them in the way they should go. This is simply because their husbands were not fulfilling that role for whatever reason. When their husbands suddenly starts taking the lead in this, it can make the wife feel as if they are no longer important or valuable in the spiritual process of the home. Do not let the enemy come against you in this. Submit to your husband's authority and come alongside him as he leads and guides the family. It does not mean your role in teaching and admonishing your children with the spiritual aspects of their lives is over. It means that you now work together with your husband toward the same goal, which is falling passionately in love with Jesus and showing your children the way they should go and do the same.

I am sure glad Jesus didn't adopt this mindset of "I will when they do" when it came to Him giving his life as a sacrifice for us on the cross. Otherwise, we would all be doomed. Life is about doing what God calls and expects us to do. We are not in marriage so that everything is fair. We are in this marriage to love our spouses. I encourage you, ladies, to read 1 Corinthians 13. It never says love is *fair*. It says love is patient and kind. Love does not seek to get its own way. When you decide to set aside selfish motives, you set the tone for a marriage that can blossom and grow into the design that God originally created. A byproduct of letting go of selfish motives is that, usually, your spouse will very quickly follow suit.

### B. Characteristic No. 2: She Watches Her Adornment So It Doesn't Become Vanity.

*1 Peter 3:3 NIV[11]*
*3 Your beauty should not come from outward adornment, such as elaborate hairstyles and the wearing of gold jewelry or fine clothes.*

There are those who take verse 3 to say that a woman should not wear makeup, braid their hair, or wear jewelry. These scriptures are not meant to be a prohibition against such items. Rather, they are placing them in their proper order.

I believe in the theory: *If the barn needs painting, paint it!*

I like for my wife to look pretty, I love her hair and the jewelry she wears. But the outward beauty of our wives, or women in general, should not be the only thing that causes an attraction. The attraction to someone can and will fade. What is from within a person is the true test of their beauty.

Peter is suggesting that these adornments not be the only beauty a woman holds, nor should they be something used to misrepresent her or her relationship with Jesus. If you are wearing something or doing something for your body that you would not mind Jesus knowing about or looking at, then keep it up. If you would not feel godly about your appearance in front of Jesus, you should change it. Real beauty comes from within, not from without. That is what Peter is saying in these verses of scripture. Many women are beautiful on the outside, but when you get to know them, you find out they have a nasty temper, or they talk behind people's backs, or they are selfish beyond measure. It is the *content and intentions of the heart* that will make a woman truly beautiful.

Let me ask you, how long would it take you to get ready for a wedding? An hour? Perhaps two? Now, do you spend that same amount of time with the Lord working on preparing and beautifying your heart and your motives before Him? If we're being honest, most women would say no. But this is exactly what Peter is getting at in these verses. Why are you so concerned with outside appearances? You may be beautiful by the world's standards, but your Christlike example looks terrible.

Did you know that the statistics for a man staying with a woman who is less attractive on the outside, but she possesses qualities like selflessness and kindness, are far greater than a man staying with a woman who only possesses outward beauty? Why is this? It's because outward beauty will fade. But a woman who continues to grow in the attributes that Jesus says are so attractive (as stated in 1 Corinthians 13) is what will hold your man's heart until one or the other of you takes your final breath.

---

> Modesty is not simply about personal preference or style. It is about love, respect, and protecting the heart of one's marriage. Unfortunately, there are women who have the attitude of dressing to please themselves rather than thinking of the implications it will have on their husbands and the people around them. We live in a culture where it is acceptable, and even encouraged, for women to

flaunt themselves and show off *what they've got*. My question is, why would a married woman want to flaunt herself, showing cleavage or their behinds, with no apparent care or concern for how their husband might feel about it? Not to mention, drawing attention from men who are not their husbands.

This is not only tacky, but shows that there is a blatant insecurity in their hearts. If it's not enough to have attention from your husband, who you should be dressing up for (or undressing for), that you have to go and do the same thing for all the world to see, then there is a serious issue here. It is not loving to your husband or Jesus to dress immodestly in public.

Some wives may argue, "Well, if they don't want to see it, then they shouldn't look. Why do I have to change the way I dress just because men are the way they are?"

That thought process is also incredibly selfish. Men are wired differently from women. That is just a fact. It's the way God made them. Men are visual. They are wired to see a woman and appreciate her beauty. This next sentiment is very controversial but it is our job as women to protect them. It is not loving and protective when we dress to show too much skin, or parts of our bodies that should be for our husbands' eyes only.

You can still dress flatteringly without having to give away the whole story, if you know what I mean. Your body is not your own anymore. You belong to your husband, just as he belongs to you. If you have a problem with that, then there is an even deeper issue you need to go after, which we will talk about further in Chapter 15, *I Own You.*

— NICOLE BOYD

---

## C. Characteristic No. 3: She Always Checks Her Attitude Before She Speaks.

*I Peter 3:4 NIV[11]*
*4 Rather, it should be that of your inner self, the unfading beauty of a gentle and quiet spirit, which is of great worth in God's sight.*

Peter says external beauty is temporary, but internal beauty is eternal. One is attractive to the world; the other is attractive to God. Peter describes this inner beauty as a gentle and quiet spirit that is precious in the sight of the Lord.

Most women do not want to hear the truth that the feminist movement is anti-God and anti-scripture. It has become very prevalent in the last several decades. Women who ascribe to this movement are mad at men and God. As a Christian woman, you need to check your attitude and actions.

Let me give you the best-kept secret in a marriage: nagging doesn't work, mainly because your attitude is wrong. Proverbs 19:13 sums up what God has to say about nagging. *"A quarrelsome or nagging wife goes on like a constant dripping."*

When women disregard modesty and pursue attention through outward display of themselves, they miss the deeper calling of cultivating a spirit that honors both God and their husbands. In the previous section, we talked to the men about being willing to receive direction from their wives. I want to touch on the flip side here. If your husband is willing to listen to advice and correction from you, you will ruin this if you try to bombard him with too many things at once. This concept has been taught in *Women are Like Spaghetti and Men are Like Waffles* by Bill and Pam Farrel, men think in boxes, one thing at a time, women think in noodles, with everything touching. We ladies tend to get a little change-happy and think, "Oh, if he's changing how he speaks to me in this area, why don't I just pile it all on and we can get it all fixed at once?"

Men do not work that way. Men need time to work on one or two things at a time, not seventy thousand. If you throw too many things at him at once, he will shut down and not do anything. Be patient and willing to show grace as he is working on himself. Cheer him on and bring encouragement when possible. We need to be our husband's biggest fans.

— NICOLE BOYD

D. **Characteristic No. 4: She Always Shows Him Respect and Makes Him No. 1.**

*I Peter 3:5-6 NIV[11]*
*5 For this is the way the holy women of the past who put their hope in God used to adorn themselves. They submitted themselves to their own husbands, 6 like Sarah, who obeyed Abraham and called him her lord. You are her daughters if you do what is right and do not give way to fear.*

The fact that Sarah called her husband *lord* speaks volumes about their relationship. It shows that she respected him, revered him, and honored him. In giving Abraham this kind of honor and attention, she was giving honor and attention to God.

Peter asks the question, "Wives, are you patterning your life after Sarah's model?" Your husband should be at the top of your list, whether he is a Christian or not. He should have the bulk of your attention and affection. Does he?

But think for a moment, who are you living for? Is it for yourself? Is it for your husband? Or is it for God?

Let's do a little analysis, ladies:

- Say out loud one thing that you respect about your husband.
- What have you done recently to show him he's your main focus and desire?
- When was the last time he got all of your undivided attention?

- What do you feel about Sarah's model? List some things from Scripture that describe her.

---

I have heard it said that Sarah is an Old Testament model, so her example and wifely characteristics are not relevant to the New Testament. However, Peter references her in the New Testament, thus validating her model as something that we still should be following. Remember, Jesus came to fulfill the Law, the Old Testament Covenant, not abolish it. Sarah and many of the Old Testament women are referenced in Hebrews 11 for their faith and how their character was credited to them as righteousness. They are women of faith and honor whose example we can build our life upon.

— NICOLE BOYD

---

### E. Characteristic No. 5: She Always Praises Him Publicly.

You may remember this point from the men's section. It goes both ways, my friends. If your husband is building walls, it stems back to the way you treat and respect him. Are you belittling him? Are you sarcastic with your responses to him? Do you see him as the boy he was when you got married, or the man he has since grown into?

I'd like to touch on the concept of not grumbling or complaining about your husbands a little more deeply. My husband is very fun-loving and energetic. Because of his somewhat *wild side*, he tends to get remarks about how obnoxious he can be. He tended to get these more frequently when he was younger, but they still come from time to time. There are times when friends or even family members have commented on his nature, or how I might need a break from him every once in a while. I do not need a break from him. He is my best friend and I love him with all my heart.

I am, by nature, not a very confrontational person. Honestly, I'd rather take a fork to the eye than have a confrontation. It's something I am working on, but I still have a difficult time with it. One night, my husband and I were hanging out with some of our family members and friends. They were teasing him, then looked at me and said something to the effect that, "I only married him for their sake". I said nothing. My husband got very quiet, and we went through the rest of the evening. When we got in the car, I could tell something was wrong, because, he is only quiet when something is wrong. I asked him if he was okay. He asked me, "Do you even want to be with me? Am I just a scum-sucking pig you put up with?" I was blindsided by this and quickly told him that that was not the case at all. He then asked me, "Do you realize you said *nothing* back there?"

I realized that it didn't matter that I was not the instigator of the complaints or what I thought were harmless barbs our friends and family were throwing at him. I stayed silent, which was just as bad as if I'd agreed with them or started the remarks in the first place.

I learned a very valuable lesson that night. *Your husband needs to know you are on his side.* Instead of remaining silent, I should have jumped to his defense. Later that night, with what became a very long discussion, he said, "You didn't have to do it in an angry way, or anything like that. You could have just said the opposite of what they were saying and kept on having fun through the evening. Just say what is true."

He doesn't need me to defend him physically. But emotionally, it hurt that I had not turned around the barbs that were coming at him. I was not a shield. I was not a safe place for him in that moment. I had left him out in the open to deal with the barbs all on his own. And while they were in jest, and he knew that, it had hurt him deeply that I hadn't tried to vindicate or stick up for him.

This was a powerful lesson learned. Sometimes we forget that men need to be praised and encouraged just as much as women. Even though I'm a non-confrontational person, that doesn't mean I wouldn't defend my family to the death, and that includes my husband. From this experience, I learned that words are powerful, even the words that *aren't* said. How can we lift up and encourage our husbands?

— NICOLE BOYD

---

**Regular Tune-Ups Make the Marriage Run Smoothly**

So what is it that you need to work on in yourself? Do you really want to save your marriage, to become a man or woman who is loving and can be loved? It will take work and time, but I assure you, becoming the person your spouse deserves is far better than starting over with someone else. Here is the last hard truth I have for you: no matter how far or fast you run, your marriage problems will follow you, because it's not your spouse that's the problem. It's YOU.

> *"There are no 'married people problems.'*
> *Only 'single people problems' carried into marriage."*
> —Jonathan Pakluda, *Outdated*

I know it sounds harsh, but that should be very comforting, because you are the only person you have control over. Start making the changes that are needed and see what happens. You would be surprised at what God can do with a submitted and obedient heart as you begin the marriage tune-up.

# MARRIAGE ACTIVATION 5

Marriage must be built on more than sexual attraction. The best marriages are built on strong friendship with one another. Take a few minutes to sit down together and answer these questions honestly.

**Are We Friends?**

1. What experience do you love to share?
2. What was the one thing that attracted you to your spouse?
3. Out of the characteristics both for the man and woman, what did you learn that you didn't know before?
4. What could you do to become a better friend with your spouse?

5. Look up a scripture in your Bible or on your phone that references the importance of marriage being a friendship and explain that verse.

## PART 2
COVENANT

*"You're still my first love,
You're still my only one..."*
**—Kari Jobe, "First Love"**

# CHAPTER 6

## THE PURPOSE OF A COVENANT

Covenant is a word that is not used often in our culture today. Certainly, we have heard this word in the church, but what does it actually mean, and how does it affect a marriage?

*Covenant[12]: a written agreement or promise usually under seal between two or more parties especially for the performance of some action*

A covenant, in the Biblical standpoint, was a promise, and there was usually a sacrifice involved. Examples from scripture include the Noahic Covenant, where God promised He would never flood the earth again. God made a covenant with Abraham. Animals were cut in two (blood sacrifice), and God moved between the pieces. God reestablished the Abrahamic covenant with Isaac and Jacob, and the people of Israel, after coming out of slavery in

Egypt. Entering into a covenant would cost each party something.

It is no different with marriage. When you get married, it's not just a piece of paper that makes up some man-made license. It is meant to be a solemn and lifelong vow, not just between the two of you, but between you, your spouse, and God. It is not to be entered into lightly, as many marriage sermons say from the very beginning of the ceremony. Oftentimes, when God either made a covenant or renewed a covenant with His people, some kind of memorial was set up to remind each party about the promises that were made (stones in the middle of the Jordan River, an altar, a rainbow in the sky). It gave them something to look back on when they were tempted to go against the confines of the covenant.

As in marriage, your relationship with God is a covenant, one that He made all the sacrifices for on the outset. He took all the risk before we ever made a decision to follow Him. But there are stipulations He expects us to abide by when we do come to Him. There are expectations He wants us to follow to fulfill our end of the covenant. He laid down his life to redeem us from sin and death. It is up to us whether we accept that sacrifice and become joined with Him in relationship through salvation. We can choose to live our lives by the conditions of the New Covenant. Living our lives for Jesus, and allowing Him to change us as we walk with Him, is called sanctification.

The marriage *ceremony/covenant* is much the same as a memorial stone would have been back in Biblical times. It is a time we can look back on and remember, hopefully with fondness, the day we pledged our lives to each other.

When things get rough, that memorial stone reminds us of the vows we made to our spouse. Also, this is the reason for the ring. The ring, which is symbolic of an endless circle, is a memorial that our love, commitment, and covenant are never to be broken from the moment we put that ring on, until death.

I want you to think back on the moment you gave your heart to Jesus, when you were *really and truly* saved. What was that moment like? I want you both to think back on that time and remember. What were you feeling? What were you thinking? Why was that moment so important and significant to you?

Covenants are legally binding. That's why there should be both positives and negatives that are put in the marriage vows. For richer or **poorer.** In **sickness** *and* in health. In good times *and* in **bad.** If we said anything like this, we have to remember the covenant is in the negative things that come against us as well as the positives. When you go through the negative, that's when your vow is proven. A battery needs a positive and a negative charge to give it power. It is when we walk through those hard times that our covenant is tested, strengthened, and validated. Thus, because of the positives and the negatives of marriage, it has true, godly power.

I want you to think about the moment when you knew God told you that you were supposed to marry the person that you had been dating and falling in love with. When did you know *this is the one,* and that you would be spending the rest of your life with them? If you are engaged and therefore not married yet, I want you to think back on the moment God told you this was your soulmate and your life partner. Whenever I am in a counseling session with couples, whether pre-marital or marital counseling, I always ask this question. If one or both of the spouses cannot tell me of that moment, I ask them to start praying for God to give them that monument in their lives.

One of the covenant monuments that God gave to my wife and me happened shortly after we started spending time together. We were standing outside the car one night. I told her that I was starting to fall in love with her and that I wanted her to be the woman I spent the rest of my life with. At that moment, she looked up into the sky and saw a shooting star, the first one she had ever seen in her life. She burst into tears, and knew that God was speaking to her that she would be my wife someday.

Life ebbs and flows. It is in those hard times that God gives us these covenant monuments to hold onto. Because it's not a question of *if* hard times will come, it's *when*.

If you are married, and having a difficult time, then I would like to ask *you* this. Has God changed His mind? Did He really tell you to marry this person, and if so, do you think there is anything that would make Him change His mind?

If you have reached this place and are making excuses as to why that may be the case, I would like to encourage you to read this next section of verses very carefully:

*Matthew 19:1-9 NIV*[10]
*1 When Jesus had finished saying these things, he left Galilee and went into the region of Judea to the other side of the Jordan. 2 Large crowds followed him, and he healed them there. 3 Some Pharisees came to him to test*

*him. They asked, "Is it lawful for a man to divorce his wife for any and every reason?"* ***4*** *"Haven't you read," he replied, "that at the beginning the Creator 'made them male and female,'* ***5*** *and said, 'For this reason a man will leave his father and mother and be united to his wife, and the two will become one flesh'?* ***6*** *So they are no longer two, but one flesh. Therefore what God has joined together, let no one separate."* ***7*** *"Why then," they asked, "did Moses command that a man give his wife a certificate of divorce and send her away?"* ***8*** *Jesus replied, "Moses permitted you to divorce your wives because your hearts were hard. But it was not this way from the beginning.* ***9*** *I tell you that anyone who divorces his wife, except for sexual immorality, and marries another woman commits adultery.*

Your issue is not necessarily that God didn't say so. The issue is your hardness of heart. Where did you allow your heart to grow hard against your spouse? What are you using as excuses to validate your desire to walk away from this marriage? Would they stand up in God's court as valid reasons for divorce?

## Two Are Better Than One

Two coffees are better than one. Two arms are better than one. I know I'm making light, but this is a truth that gets overlooked so often. God did not call you to a marriage so you could feel just as alone as when you were single. The issue now is you've got double the problems and double the heartache to deal with. In marriage, you were supposed to work together, to work as a team. So, where has the breakdown manifested from?

> *Ecclesiastes 4:9-12 NIV[13]*
> *9 Two are better than one,*
>   *because they have a good return for their labor:*
> *10 If either of them falls down,*
>   *one can help the other up.*
> *But pity anyone who falls*
>   *and has no one to help them up.*
> *11 Also, if two lie down together, they will keep warm.*
>   *But how can one keep warm alone?*
> *12 Though one may be overpowered,*
>   *two can defend themselves.*
> *A cord of three strands is not quickly broken.*

So if you have heard from God that you were supposed to marry your spouse, and you know now that He has not changed His mind (Matthew 19), then where do you go from here? Is there a hardness of heart that needs to be dealt with? Or perhaps expectations, that need to be reevaluated and adjusted in your heart and life? In many cases, this means letting go of unfair expectations and pre-conceived notions of what marriage was going to look like. This means we have to take a hard look at what your marriage currently is, and start to do the maintenance and the rebuilding needed to make it run smoothly.

I would like to share with you what I like to call *The Ten Guidelines of Marriage*, five for the ladies and five for the men. We will begin with the ladies.

# The Five Guidelines for Wives

1. ## Give up on Your Desire for the Perfect Marriage

Marriage is the most difficult and complex of all human relationships. It requires patience, skill, tact, emotional growth and continual spiritual growth. You can grow a good marriage only if you are willing to work at it.

Maybe we need to adopt the philosophy of the woman who responded when the pastor asked if she took her husband for better or worse. She said, "He can't get much worse, and there ain't no hope of him getting any better, so I take him as he is." It takes a wise and patient wife to make a good husband. They seldom come ready-made.

2. ## Give Up On All Hope of Changing Your Husband Through Criticism or Sarcasm

The simple truth is, you cannot make your husband more thoughtful by complaining. Such tactics usually have one of two results with men. They will either retreat and build a wall, or they will become hostile and abusive.

We can change no one other than ourselves by direct action. We can only change ourselves. And when we change, others tend to change in reaction to us. Believe this in faith, not in visible evidence. Remember, faith is the substance of things hoped for, the evidence of things not yet seen (Hebrews 11:1). Give up making demands. Abandon the martyr/victim mentality and don't embellish the truth to make yourself look like you're being treated worse than you are. Begin to be what you want him to be for you. This is where believing in faith begins.

### 3. Give Praise and Affection (Instead of Seeking it)

*Ephesians 4:29 NKJV[14]*
*29 "Let no corrupt word proceed out of your mouth, but what is good for necessary edification, that it may impart grace to the hearers."*

Be your husband's biggest fan. Remember the story that Nicole talked about, not sticking up for her husband with his friends and family? Your husband has deep needs to be admired. He wants to know if you value him, if you respect what he does, and if you are proud of him.

If your friends only knew your husband by what they heard *you* say about him, what would they think? When you're around your women friends, don't rag on your husband. *Brag* on your husband. Say good things about him to others. And when you do, *mean it*. It will pay dividends in your relationship. Remember this verse because it comes into play very heavily here: do unto your husband as you would have him to do unto you (Luke 6:31). We call it the Golden Rule, and this should be the foundation of all marriages.

### 4. Do Things Your Husband Loves to Do.

*Ecclesiastes 4:9-10 NKJV[13]*
*9 Two are better than one,*
*Because they have a good reward for their labor.*
*10 For if they fall, one will lift up his companion.*
*But woe to him who is alone when he falls,*
*For he has no one to help him up.*

Guys want their wives to be their best friends. They want to hang out with them. They want their wives to share in their interests. You already know the answer to this, but I want you to say it out loud. If there is one thing your husband likes to do on this earth, what is that? It could be going hunting, riding motorcycles or horses, fishing, or watching sports. Do you do that with him?

Enjoy time with your husband. Develop the intimacy that comes from having fun together. Stop convincing yourself that his hobby is only a part of his world and that you don't have to be a part of it. That is a lie from the enemy. I guarantee you, if you start taking an interest in that thing your husband loves, you will see a side of your husband that you have never seen before.

---

When Colton and I first got married, I had no grid for anything that had to do with archery. I had no idea how to even hold a bow, much less shoot it. I came from a family that was very much *not* into hunting, and that's fine. But when I entered the Boyd family, I wanted to try things that were important to Colton and my new family. We bought a starter bow for me on our honeymoon, because I told him I wanted to try. I couldn't promise that I would fall in love with archery like he had, but I was willing to give it a go.

A month after our wedding, we went on our first hunting trip as a married couple. I was so stoked when I shot my first buck. We called him Rambo Buck because he was bound and determined to get away. After four arrows, we finally got him on the ground, and I was so excited about my first little spike buck.

It turned into quite the adventure because I had no idea what I was doing, but Colton was there to coach me through everything. I ended up falling in love with hunting and being in the woods, camping and hiking, which is something we get to share as a couple and as a family. I would have never known I loved those things if I hadn't tried them. So, ladies, even if you don't know if something is your *thing,* can I encourage you to be willing to try? Whatever it is that your husband likes to do, be willing to meet him where he is and just *try*. You may find it's not your thing, but maybe there is a way you can still meet him halfway. Go camping with him, even if you don't hunt, for example. No matter if you end up liking that hobby and get involved, or simply go with him as an observer, I promise you, you will be pleased with the outcome because you will be building intimacy by caring about what he cares about.

— NICOLE BOYD

## 5. Provide a Peaceful Sanctuary

*Proverbs 17:1 NIV*[15]
*1 Better a dry crust with peace and quiet
than a house full of feasting, with strife.*

Would you say that your home is a stress-reducing or stress-producing place? Is it a sanctuary? I know that it can be difficult to create a peaceful, loving environment, especially in this society of two-career families. In no way am I suggesting that it is the wife's sole responsibility to turn her house into a stress-free home. It is a team effort. However, how you view the word sanctuary does come into play here. Sanctuary is more than just the main part of a church building. It is defined as a place of refuge and protection.

Can you honestly say that this word defines your home? Just remember that the first few minutes inside the door set the tone for the rest of the evening. Meet him at the door and welcome him. Make your home a place that is a refuge from the rest of the world and a place of protection that everyone who enters feels loved, appreciated, and safe.

Don't meet him at the door with the news that Jimmy has been bad, the sink is backed up, and the bank called and you're bank account is overdrawn. How would it change the atmosphere of your home if you greeted him with a kiss, asked him about his day, and then started telling him about yours? Then, what if you just took a few minutes to pray together before anything else happened? It is not about controlling the mood of the home, or tiptoeing around issues to keep the peace. But you are an instrumental part of making that home a sanctuary and a place of peace.

**The Five Guidelines For Husbands**

*1 Peter 3:7 NIV[11]*
*7 Husbands, in the same way be considerate as you live with your wives, and treat them with respect as the weaker partner and as heirs with you of the gracious gift of life, so that nothing will hinder your prayers.*

Men, listen carefully; this may be the most important piece of advice that you will ever receive concerning your marriage. If you want bonus points with your wife today, make sure you prioritize listening to her and really being concerned and attentive.

1. **Don't Take Your Marriage and Your Wife For Granted**

*Ephesians 5:25 NIV[9]*
*25 Husbands, love your wives, just as Christ loved the church and gave himself up for her.*

Don't take your marriage or your wife for granted. There are so many small, unspoken ways that you can help her around the house that tell her you are engaged in everything she does and in what is important to her. Some men actually seem to believe that God created Adam and noticed all the leftover fruit rinds lying around the garden and created a woman to pick them up. One woman said that her husband's idea of helping out was to lift his feet when she was vacuuming. Maybe that's why God created the robo-vacuum.

Guys, we need to put our relationship with our spouse back at the top of the list. So, where do you think your wife would say she falls on your priority list? What are the things that she would list off that she is in competition with?

### 2. Communication is Not A Bad Word

In Proverbs 16:24 (NKJV), we find these wise words of advice, *"Pleasant words are like a honeycomb, Sweetness to the soul and health to the bones."*[16]

Husbands, you need to work at verbalizing your feelings for your wife. You need to tell her how you feel. This is not always natural for men. Remember how it was when you were dating? That's why she fell in love with you. If you take out the communication for a woman, you have taken out what feeds her soul.

My wife will never make a decision about anything until it is talked over from every angle and direction—multiple times. I have learned that this is not a bad process. There have been many possible mistakes and mishaps avoided from this angle-and-direction communication process. I never realized it was so valuable when I was single. By slowing life down and communicating through all of the different variables and contexts, I've learned to appreciate her way. Instead of the bull-in-the-china-shop, we chose the talking-canaries-at-the-coffee-shop approach.

My husband values this approach of the talking-canaries-at-the-coffee-shop way more than I do. The reason for stating that is that not every marriage can be typecast with the women as the talkers and men as the listeners. Some women are verbal processors, while some are not. I personally would love to not talk and just drink coffee at the coffee shop, but that approach doesn't work either. I'm more of a bury-it-until-you-explode kind of communicator. Explosions are messy. I have learned over the years of being married to a verbal processor to voice my feelings before I ever get close to spewing my anger all over him and the others that surround me.

No matter where you fall in this example, whether you're the talker or the listener, communication is vital in making every marriage healthy.

— NICOLE BOYD

### 3. Not Every Problem Needs a Solution.

*James 1:19 NIV[17]*
*19b ...take note of this: Everyone should be quick to listen, slow to speak and slow to become angry...*

A common complaint from women is that their husbands don't listen to them and understand them. The men, on the other hand, are bewildered and say, "I do listen to her! The problem is she uses so many words that I can't think fast enough to remember what she's really trying to say." What is typically happening is the woman wants to talk about a problem and share how she is feeling about it. The man wants to get the problem solved and over with as quickly as possible—just to stop more words from coming out.

The conversations may go something like this.

The woman says, "I had a terrible day at work."

The man says, "Well, why don't you quit?"

The woman says, "I didn't say I wanted to quit. I was just trying to tell you I had a hard day."

He says, "If you didn't want my opinion, why did you ask for it?"

She says, "Just forget I said anything."

He says, "Okay, I will."

For the next week, try to listen to your wife, let her know you understand how she feels, and don't try to fix the situation unless she asks you to. I cannot emphasize this enough, so much of our lives comes through proper and healthy communication. How someone feels may not always be expressed by what they say. It's by the *way* they say it! As husbands, listening is critical here. Your wife may want to just express something by sharing it, without the fear of you feeling responsible for fixing it. Verbalizing something often takes the power away. For example, talking about a fearful thought helps her to process what she's truly feeling before her emotions get the better of her. When you bring something out of the dark and into the light, it loses the power to control you.

### 4. Avoid Criticism

***Proverbs 13:3 NIV*[18]**
*Those who guard their lips preserve their lives,*
  *but those who speak rashly will come to ruin.*

We discussed with the ladies earlier about honor and respect for your husbands with protecting and defending them. The same goes for you, men. Criticizing and humiliating your wife for not reaching your expectations will only cause more distance and resentment. A critical person is someone people don't want to be around—especially if they are stuck being married to them. Remember the emotional bank account? It takes five positive compliments to erase one critical withdrawal?

What if, instead of voicing your frustration with a constant barrage of criticism, you tried walking in your wife's shoes first? In this culture, where most families have two people working outside the home, it can be a real downer for your wife to have to come home from a long day at her job, and then feel like her work is just beginning. She's got to clean the house, cook dinner, pack lunches for the kids, make sure everyone's homework is done, do the laundry, and prep the clothes for the next day. The list seems to go on and on. It can be very isolating when she feels like she has no help from her husband, who, by the way, was supposed to be her helpmate. Being a helpmate goes both ways. Jealousy and resentment can enter so easily. Now, when you add in here your current biggest criticism of her, and you can see why she might be struggling...

## 5. Remember the Little Things Really Do Matter

As men, we have a huge tendency to become way too lazy and choose not to take responsibility for why we missed something small and insignificant that is important to our wives. By this, I mean anniversaries, birthdays, special dating memories, and simple milestones in your life together. These things are way bigger than any man could ever realize or appreciate, so you will need to be intentional in your approach to this. For example, my wife and I fondly remember the night of our first kiss. We know exactly where we were and what prompted that moment. I have, throughout our marriage, sent her little texts or notes letting her know how important that date is to me. This always creates a positive outcome—if you know what I mean.

―――

As you can see from these ten guidelines for marriage, a covenant comes with give and take. These aren't necessarily concrete conditions for your marriage. But if you want a *good* marriage, then start by doing your part, regardless of your spouse's performance in facilitating what you need or want. The bottom line for understanding a covenant is this: *God is making a promise or provision to mankind, and in return, He is expecting man to make a commitment, obligation, or promise back to Him.*

> "A covenant is an unchangeable, divinely imposed legal agreement between God and man that stipulates the conditions of their relationship."
> —Wayne Grudem

Within the marriage covenant, there is a similar expectation. There are guidelines (those presented above) that make up the DNA of every marriage. These guidelines are the binding spiritual epoxy which binds them together *for better or worse, richer or poorer, in sickness and in health, until death do they part*. We must realize that within our marriage, there are common denominators to this covenant. We make a promise to our spouse to love, honor, and cherish them. And in return, our spouse expects us to make a commitment, obligation, and promise back to them forever.

I would like to propose an expansion of the above definition of a covenant:

> *"A covenant is an unchangeable, divinely imposed legal agreement between God, man, and his spouse (woman) through the bond of holy matrimony that stipulates the conditions of their relationship."*
> -Jim Boyd (through the inspiration of Wayne Grudem)

A covenant must have the participation of all parties, or else it is invalid. Hence, the reason I included God, man, and his spouse. The Word talks about the *three-stranded cord*, and how much a binding agreement cannot be easily broken. You must have God at the center, but you must also have the willing agreement and participation from each spouse.

## A Divine Promise

> *Matthew 5:37 NIV[19]*
> *37 All you need to say is simply 'Yes' or 'No'; anything beyond this comes from the evil one.*

What does a covenant represent? The original Hebrew literally means *to cut*. A biblical contract was made into a covenant and fulfilled in the Old Testament by cutting an animal in half. Then, the two individuals who were binding themselves to that legal contract would walk between the two halves of the sacrifice to visualize the promise they had agreed to. This was done in order for witnesses to be present who would verify and validate the original covenant terms. The reason for the severity of this visible covenant was to declare the seriousness of the covenant and its ever-binding nature. It said, "If I do not fulfill my end of this covenant promise, then may my life become as this sacrifice."

In marriage, on the wedding night, blood is also spilled. Blood would have been evidence of the final bond of covenant between this man and woman, until death parted them. This is the visible seal between the two of them before God. No one else can ever create or re-create the covenant they made on that night.

# MARRIAGE ACTIVATION 6

The covenant is the bedrock that your marriage is built on. Without a deep commitment to your spouse, marriage might as well be just another piece of paper, as so many are fond of stating in our modern culture. Throughout these activities and questions, really examine your heart to see where you stand in your mindset and actions.

1. Why is the marriage covenant such a misunderstood process in our modern culture? Why did God create a covenant between Himself and man, which was later illustrated through the marriage process?
2. When was the moment you heard God say that you were supposed to marry your spouse? Write it down and give specific details.

3. Take some time to remember with your spouse how God told you that your spouse was the one you were supposed to marry. This can be a fun and healing exercise to hear and remember how God told your spouse that you were the one for them and vice versa.
4. Take a few minutes after you've discussed the importance of your marriage vows together and pray for God's favor and blessing in your future. Both of you take turns to pray.

# CHAPTER 7

## THE POWER OF A COVENANT

The Jewish wedding ceremony is rich in detail and filled with deep spiritual symbolism. At its heart, it celebrates two individuals—often from different backgrounds, families, perspectives, or even parts of the world—coming together as one. The steps involved in this covenant ceremony reflect God's original design for marriage and offer valuable lessons we can apply to our own relationships. Over the years, during my tours and travels in Israel, I've had many conversations with local friends about their festivals, customs, and traditions. Interestingly, when the topic of weddings comes up, each one has remarked—independently—that Western wedding ceremonies have lost much of their solemnity and tradition.

Marriage will cost you something, but in the Jewish wedding ceremony, the wedding itself will cost you greatly. By the end of the ceremonies, the couple will have gone through months, if not years, of hard work, money, and preparation. This is meant to reveal the intentions of the heart. Do you really want to go through this much work, conflict resolution, and discomfort to marry this person? Do you actually mean the promise of your future to this person? We must keep in mind the intensity and severity of how God looks at the wedding vows and understand the purpose of a marriage covenant. This wedding ceremony is not just a contract, but a covenant that is intended to seal the marriage between the two parties forever.

There is a new slang term being used in our Western culture that validates why this is being overlooked. That term is "first marriage." There is even a sitcom show currently running using this name. What is being said is that everyone will have a first marriage, where they can make all their mistakes and iron out their flaws, which will prepare them for their second, real marriage.

This is not God's plan or desire for marriage. But somehow, our Western culture has become accepting of this model over the last fifty to sixty years. People try to get married on the cheapest plan possible, and in any place except the church. Why is this? In part, it is the feeling of seriousness that having the wedding in the church brings along with it. If we stand in a church and promise ourselves to one another in front of all these people, and it doesn't work out, then we lied. We do not want to have to sacrifice or be called liars later in order to get married. But in the Jewish custom of marriage, preparing for this special day is part of growing together as a couple toward a common goal. The preparation for the wedding becomes preparation for the future of their marriage, their lives, and their own family yet to come.

It is vital to have an understanding of the solemnity of

the wedding ceremony, and in some way, bring back the seriousness of the wedding ceremony into this culture so we can build it into the next generations.

The wedding ceremony in the Jewish culture is so much more than a fun party—and believe you me, they throw an amazing party. It is an ancient ritual that not only carries an immense weight of responsibility for the husband and wife, but points prophetically to the coming Messiah and the amazing celebration we all get to be a part of at the Marriage Supper of the Lamb that the Bible talks about in Revelation 19:

> *Revelation 19:6-9 ESV[20]*
> ***The Marriage Supper of the Lamb***
> ***6*** *Then I heard what seemed to be the voice of a great multitude, like the roar of many waters and like the sound of mighty peals of thunder, crying out, "Hallelujah! For the Lord our God the Almighty reigns.* ***7*** *Let us rejoice and exult and give him the glory, for the marriage of the Lamb has come, and his Bride has made herself ready;* ***8*** *it was granted her to clothe herself with fine linen, bright and pure"—for the fine linen is the righteous deeds of the saints.* ***9*** *And the angel said to me, "Write this: Blessed are those who are invited to the marriage supper of the Lamb." And he said to me, "These are the true words of God."*

Let's dive into the significance of each of the parts of the Jewish wedding ceremony, and see how we can apply these to our own marriage covenants.

In Hebrew, the Jewish wedding is called a *simcha* שִׂמְחָה

(or a joyous occasion). These joyous celebrations were a command, where the bride and groom's family and friends were commanded to add to the couple's joy by singing, dancing, and feasting. This was not just a suggestion. It was expected.

> *Jeremiah 33:11 NIV[21]*
> *11 the sounds of joy and gladness, the voices of bride and bridegroom, and the voices of those who bring thank offerings to the house of the Lord, saying,*
> *"Give thanks to the Lord Almighty,*
> *for the Lord is good;*
> *his love endures forever."*
> *For I will restore the fortunes of the land as they were before,' says the Lord.*

Do you still have the joy of your first love? Or are you and your spouse simply going through the motions? This is a terrible tragedy caused by stripping the seriousness of a wedding ceremony by our Western culture. We do not find joy in our marriages anymore. We do not celebrate the small things. When you look back on your wedding day, do you remember the words that were said? Or did it all seem to pass in a daze? Unfortunately, I am guilty of this in my own marriage. I am glad we have a wedding video to look back on, but part of me wishes we had been able to slow down and really enjoy the moments without feeling rushed to get through everything so we could get on to the honeymoon. The wedding ceremony is not just something to get through, but something to be able to look back on as a memorial stone for the future.

There are three distinct parts to an ancient Jewish wedding: the *shiddukhin* (mutual agreement), *erusin* (engagement), and the *nissuin* (marriage).

## The Shiddukhin (The Promise)

*Genesis 2:18 NIV[1]*
*18 The Lord God said, "It is not good for the man to be alone. I will make a helper suitable for him."*

The *shiddukhin* refers to the arrangements that take place prior to the legal betrothal. It is the mutual promise between a man and a woman to marry at a future time, essentially setting themselves apart for one another. This is the part where the negotiations of the dowry and the covenant contract begin.

Unlike our Western culture, the couple thought of themselves as if they were already married from this moment on. It is my encouragement to couples to start thinking about their commitment level even before they are married. Without this commitment to the marriage covenant, the relationship can be broken if one or both parties decide that things are too hard. There is even a thought process that *they aren't married yet,* so wild oats can still be sown and it will not matter. This attitude is wrong and goes completely against scripture. Even now, whether you have been married for a long time or are preparing to get married, you need to settle in your heart and spirit that you are committing to your spouse, no matter what.

## The Erusin (The Engagement)

There are several ceremonies that take place during the engagement period in a Jewish wedding. Each one builds on the seriousness of the decision that the couple is making.

### 1. The Signing of the *Ketubah*

In ancient times, the *ketubah* was put in place to protect the wife's rights. The *ketubah* specifies the responsibilities of the husband in caring for the wife and the amount of support that would be due to the wife if ever there were a divorce. The father of the groom would often select a bride for his son, just as Abraham did for Isaac in Genesis 24. In Ultra-Orthodox Judaism, many marriages are still brokered or have matchmakers to arrange them. This is still a very respected vocation today. It may sound strange to our modern minds that matchmaking is still an honored tradition. It was, and is, believed that romantic love was to develop over time. One can fall in or out of love on a whim, but a contract such as the one described above was to be the catalyst for growing in love.

Many of us have grown up with the idea that, "first comes love, then comes marriage..." In the ancient Jewish culture, marriage came first, and love blossomed from a mutual commitment to one another. Take a moment to think about your spouse using this mindset. How have you been viewing your marriage, and does anything need to change concerning your commitment level?

## 2. The *Badaken*

After the *ketubah* signing, there is a ceremony called the *badaken.* It is a short ceremony, but it is rich with meaning. During this ceremony, the groom covers the bride's face with her veil.

In this part of the process, the bride-to-be is given special consideration. In most cultures during ancient times, it was common for a woman not to be given any say in who she married. But in Jewish culture, the bride was able to accept or reject a man's proposal and enter into the arrangement willingly. Just as Rebecca was asked if she agreed to go back with Abraham's servant to become Isaac's wife, so the bride must be willing to enter into the marriage covenant agreement. This was very unusual in ancient civilizations.

The *badaken* illustrates our relationship with Jesus. We cannot be forced into a relationship with Jesus Christ, our Lord and Savior. Just as Rebecca was asked if she would go, so the Holy Spirit draws us and beckons us into a willing relationship with Him. We are joined in a covenant of love through the cross and the shedding of blood by Jesus. This is the illustration of Him as the Groom, and us, the Church, as the Bride.

In relation to our modern marriages, did you willingly agree to enter into this covenant? Or were there selfish motives involved? Did you really count the cost of what marriage would mean for you and the person you love, or did you do it to try to assuage a guilty conscience or perhaps with convenience in mind?

In ancient times, the *erusin* period would traditionally

last about a year. During this time, the groom would prepare a place for his bride by building an addition onto his father's house. The bride would also prepare herself by making her wedding garments, collecting lamps and other things needed for the wedding ceremony, as well as her new home with the groom. She knew the groom would come to call for her in about a year, but she had to be ready when he came—usually in the dead of night—or at a moment's notice. As the year of *erusin* neared completion, the bride and her attendants would even sleep in their wedding apparel, so they would be ready at a moment's notice for when the shofar would be blown to announce the groom's arrival and the final phase of the wedding covenant to begin. This is the reason the bride also kept her oil lamps trimmed and ready at all times, in case the groom called for her at night to lead the bridal procession to the home he had built and prepared for her.[22]

When the groom did come to collect his bride, she was not allowed to touch her foot on the ground. The bride was lifted up into the air on a chair and carried by the groom's attendants to the place where the final components of the wedding ceremony were to take place.

Sound familiar? In the parable of the Ten Virgins in Matthew 25, Jesus likened the Kingdom of Heaven to this special period of *erusin,* when the groom comes for his bride.

> *Matthew 25:6-7 NIV*[23]
> "At midnight the cry rang out: 'Here's the bridegroom! Come out to meet him!' Then all the virgins woke up and trimmed their lamps."

This is a prophetic declaration for the Bride of Christ (the Church and all Christians) to remain alert, as His coming could be at any moment.[25] He was also speaking to the disciples about the condition of the Church in the end times:

*Matthew 7:21 NIV[24]*
*"Not everyone who says to Me, 'Lord, Lord,' will enter the kingdom of heaven, but only he who does the will of my Father who is in heaven."*

Marriage is a picture of our relationship with Jesus Christ, the Groom. We cannot have healthy marriages without Jesus being the center of our relationship. He comes first. There is no other way to make a healthy marriage if that priority is out of order. Is this the case for you and your spouse? Have you made Jesus the center of your heart and lives as the wise virgins did, or are you going through the motions, as the five foolish virgins did in the parable?

Traditionally, in Jewish ceremonies in preparation for the betrothal ceremony in more modern settings, the bride and groom are separately immersed in water in a *mikvah*, which is a designated location agreed upon by both parties that symbolizes their spiritual cleansing in preparation for their marriage covenant. In Matthew 3, Jesus was baptized by John in the waters of *mikvah* at the Jordan River. As the Bride-to-be, we are also asked to be immersed in these waters of cleansing, and as a sign that we are married to our Beloved Savior and Lord. When we go down into the water of baptism, it symbolizes the death of our flesh, and when we come out of the water, we are raised to new life. How interesting that in a Jewish wedding, it is as if they are shedding their old lives in order to create this new life together as one new family. They cannot go back to the way things were before when they were single. They are now pursuing marriage. The things they did in singleness cannot and should not follow them into marriage, difficult as it might be. This baptism, as believers, represents that we will never be the same again, in action or in word. Just as we are joined with Christ in his suffering and raised up again, a new creation in Him, so must we step out of our old ways as a single person and create one new person, one new unit bonded together before God, surrendering our lives unto Him as a living sacrifice.

How beautiful would it be to bring this tradition back into the preparations for the wedding ceremony? Have you cut ties with the old life in preparation for your new life with your spouse? Take a moment now to search your heart and pray. Ask the Lord if there is anything—old thought patterns or selfishness—that is still clinging onto you from before you were married. Ask Him what is holding you back from being fully devoted to this covenant relationship.

The groom and his friends usually dance after the *mikvah*, in preparation for the bride and groom to enter the next phase of the wedding, the *chuppah*.

3. The *Chuppah*[25]

*Proverbs 18:22 NIV*[26]
*22 "He who finds a wife finds what is good and receives favor from the Lord."*

This is where the main ceremony begins. The wedding party enters the location where the wedding is to take place, and the guests are seated. Then, the bride and groom make their way to the central point of the ceremony—the canopy held up by four poles known as the *chuppah* (pronounced khoo-puh).

Originally, the *chuppah* cloth was draped around the bride and groom, but was later spread over their heads, with four staves at each corner, and held up by four men. In some places, a *tallit* (prayer shawl) was used to drape over the couple or was held above them. The single cloth under which the bride and groom knelt symbolized the new household being formed, which represents the public recognition of their new status as husband and wife, and using the prayer shawl illustrates God reigning over the proceedings.

There is great attention given to creating an attractive *chuppah* in accordance with the Jewish concept of *hiddur mitzvah* (embellishing the precept). It is a place that is selected for its beauty and sacredness.

Jesus Christ is our covering as we embark on this adventure called marriage. He is surely in our midst. What a beautiful representation of what our marriage relationship is supposed to be—a place that hosts the very presence of

God and points people toward Him, a place where all are welcome and can experience His love and presence.

## The Nissuin (Wedding Proper)

> *John 14:3 NIV*[27]
> *"And if I go and prepare a place for you, I will come back and take you to be with me that you also may be where I am."*

The final step in the Jewish wedding is the *nissuin,* the wedding proper. The word *nissuin* comes from the Hebrew word *naso*—to lift up. At this time, the groom has been anxiously waiting to hear from his father, who has been overseeing and helping facilitate the addition being built to his home. The son waits for the father to check off on this new building addition and declare, "Go get your bride." It is time for the wedding ceremony to go through its final steps and for him to take the bride into his house to become his wife. They will again enter the *chuppah,* recite the blessings of the wine, and finalize their vows. This is synonymous with what we read in Revelation, with Christ stating that He does not even know the day or the hour of His return. He is also waiting for his Father to announce, "Go get your Bride."

### 4. The Blessings of the Betrothal, *Kiddushin*[28]

At this point, after the bride and groom have come back under the *chuppah,* the couple drinks from two cups of wine. The wine cups are filled to express joy, with the wine representing that which can break through boundaries and reveal the hidden things in a person's heart.

This is why it was such a dire need at the wedding in Cana for Mary to come to Jesus and ask Him to intervene when the wine ran out (John 2:1-12).[29] It was deeply shameful for the wine to run out at a wedding ceremony, especially at this stage. It was also a bad sign if the wine was bitter, as it symbolized that the couple's wedding joy had, and would, run out.

After they drink the wine, the rabbi then recites two blessings.

The first blessing is this: *"Blessed are You, Lord our God, King of the Universe, Who creates the fruit of the vine."*

*John 15:5 NIV[30]*
*5 "I am the vine; you are the branches. If you remain in me and I in you, you will bear much fruit; apart from me you can do nothing."*

Our marriages are supposed to bring forth the fruit of the Spirit, and we can only do that if we are connected to the Vine, who is Jesus Christ. Are you bringing forth mature fruit in your life and marriage? If you were to ask people what they saw in your example of a married couple, what do you think would be said of you?

The second blessing: *"Blessed are You, Lord our God, King of the Universe, Who has made us holy through His commandments, and has commanded us concerning forbidden unions, forbidding us those who are betrothed, and permitting us those who are wedded to us through ĥuppa and kiddushin. Blessed are*

*You, Lord, Who sanctifies His people Israel through ĥuppa and kiddushin."*

After these blessings are recited, the rabbi gives the cup to the groom to take a sip. Then the cup is handed to the bride so she can also sip. This part of the ceremony and the blessings express the couple's resolve to create a Jewish home, dedicated to God and the well-being of all humanity.

This ceremony is reminiscent of the Last Supper, where Jesus establishes the New Covenant of grace with us. He, as the rabbi, blessed the wine and passed the cup around to his disciples so they could each take a drink. At this point, He said He would not drink of the fruit of the vine again until we all drink it together in his Kingdom at the Marriage Supper of the Lamb.

### 5. The Giving of the Ring

After the wine, it is time for the groom to give the bride an object of value, usually a ring. As custom dictates, the ring should be totally plain, without stones or markings, as it represents that the marriage should be one of simple beauty. Usually, Jewish wedding bands are inscribed with the words, *"Ani L'Dodi V'Dodi Li"* (I am my beloved's and my beloved is mine).

The circular nature of the ring represents the eternal nature of the marriage covenant. During this ceremony, the rabbi confirms that the ring belongs to the groom. He either has to purchase the ring himself, or has been given the ring as a gift—from a parent or other relative. The rabbi then confirms that the bride is willing to accept the ring, and he bids the groom place the ring on her finger. The groom then recites the following: "Behold, you are consecrated to me with this ring in accordance with the law of Moses and Israel." This concludes the *kiddushin* ceremony.

We still hold to this tradition in our Western wedding ceremonies, but I find it interesting that the rings have gotten more elaborate and costly as time has elapsed. But what about the covenant they represent? So often, these promises are thrown away at a whim, because our vows have no real cost or sacrifice. We focus so much on the *party* that we forget the true significance of what we are doing. In contrast to the ceremonies we have been studying, an American wedding ceremony can last about twenty-five to forty minutes. The reception can last anywhere from three hours to long into the night and early morning hours. It is common for people to get glaringly drunk and cause havoc, all in the name of celebrating the couple. But what about the simple beauty of what marriage is supposed to look like?

I find the ring ceremony very reminiscent of Jesus' words after his crucifixion and resurrection. He told the disciples to wait in Jerusalem for when he would send the gift of the Holy Spirit. All those who believe in Jesus are given this gift, the Seal of the Holy Spirit, as a promise that He would again return for us, His Bride. He promised that He would not leave us as orphans, and we have the Holy Spirit as the greatest and most precious gift of all to remind us of the covenant that Jesus sealed with His blood. He bought and paid for our redemption, so we could be reunited in completeness and wholeness with Him.

## 6. The Reading of the *Ketubah*

At this point in the Jewish wedding, the *ketubah* is read in the original Aramaic text and then is given to the groom. He hands it to his bride for her to hold all the days of their marriage. It is a legally binding agreement and is the property of the bride.

## 7. The *Sheva Brachot,* or Seven Blessings

Seven blessings are now recited by either the rabbi or a *chazan* (vocalist who leads people in song), or other people that the couple wants to honor. These ancient blessings set the couple into a wider social and sacred context. The blessings are as follows:

- **The Blessing of the vine/wine: symbol of joy.** *"Blessed are you, Lord our God, Ruler of the Universe, who creates the fruit of the vine."*

- **The Blessing proclaiming God to whom all creation proclaims praise.** *"Blessed are you, Lord our God, Ruler of the Universe, who created everything for His glory."*

- **God is praised, Creator of humanity.** *"Blessed are you, Lord our God, Ruler of the Universe, who created humanity."*

- **God is praised, He who created humanity in His Divine image.** *"Blessed are you, Lord our God,*

*Ruler of the Universe, who created humanity in His image, in the image of the likeness of his form, and made for them an everlasting establishment. Blessed are you, Lord, who created humanity."*

- **The Blessing for the hope of a Messianic future.** *"May the barren one (Jerusalem) rejoice greatly and delight in the ingathering of her children within her in joy. Blessed are you, Lord, who causes Zion to rejoice with her children."*

- **Prayer for the happiness of the bride and groom** *"The loving partners shall rejoice as You caused your creatures to delight in the Garden of Eden of old. Blessed are you, Lord, who causes the groom and bride to rejoice."*

- **The individual hope for happiness for the couple is combined with a prayer for joy in the Messianic future.** *"Blessed are you, Lord our God, Ruler of the Universe, who creates happiness and joy, groom and bride. Exultation, delight, amusement, and pleasure, love and brotherhood, peace and friendship. Soon, Lord our God, may the sound of happiness and the sound of joy and the voice of the groom and the voice of the bride be heard in the cities of Judah and the streets of Jerusalem — the rejoicing of groom from their chuppahs and youths from their singing banquets. Blessed are you, Lord, who makes the groom rejoice with the bride."*

As believers, we know that our Messiah has already come. And He will come again, as He said He would when He ascended into heaven to go and build a home for us.[31] Can you see how marriage is a picture of our relationship with God? The Father and His Son, the Groom, long for His Bride. He longs for intimacy with us as His chosen people. I love how these blessings speak of a return to Eden, a place where we were supposed to enjoy a full and complete, intimate relationship with God. And it's all made possible by our Beloved Groom, Jesus Christ.

## 8. The Breaking of the Glass

At the conclusion of the ceremony, it is marked by the groom stomping on a glass and smashing it under his foot. It is the official signal to cheer, dance, and shout, "Mazal Tov!" The party then commences.

But what does the smashing of the glass mean? There are several representations that have been interpreted over the years. Here are a few:

- The glass shattering is the representation of the fragility of human relationships, and a reminder that marriage will change your life (hopefully for the better), forever.
- It is a superstition that a loud noise is thought to drive away evil spirits.
- It is a break with the past. It is to be a representation that marriage is to last as long as the glass remains broken, or in other words, forever.

- It symbolizes the destruction of the Temple 2,000 years ago
- It symbolizes a hope that your children, and thus your happiness, will be as plentiful as the shards of glass now on the ground.

Once you say your vows and become man and wife, you no longer live, think, eat, or sleep the way you used to when you were single. You are wholly devoted to building a life with your spouse. All other aspects of your single life will change as you go forward now that you're married.

It is the same when we come to Jesus. We surrender our wants and desires, our dreams, and we lay them at His feet. We begin to build the life He has for us, and it is so much better than we could have ever imagined for ourselves. We enter a partnership and covenant filled with His Holy Spirit intimacy that is so much greater, broader, and deeper than we could have imagined.

Have you and your spouse broken with the things of the past, as the shattering of the glass indicates? When you say your vows and enter into this covenant, there is no going back. There is no Plan B. Have you made that conscious decision, drawn a line in the sand, and purposed in your heart that there is no other option for you?

## 9. The *Yihhud,* A Time for Private Reflection

At this point, the newlywed couple proceeds out of the ceremony area, and the final part of the order of service takes place. This part of the wedding is called the *yihhud* and is considered to be the most intimate and private ritual of the day. *Yihhud* means *oneness* or *togetherness* and speaks of unity. The couple is required to have some time alone—away from their family and friends—in order to reflect on what just took place. They go away from their guests before rejoining the celebration. In ancient times, the bride and groom would have actually consummated the marriage at this time. It is also believed that the sheet with the blood, with proof of the bride's virginity, would have been hung out of a window of the bridal chamber, to show that she came to her husband in purity and chastity. In this, blood is shed to make the covenant legally binding.

Thus, the *yihhud* was a very solemn time of reflection. After this time, the married couple would join in with the guests, and the celebration and feasting would begin.

As believers, it is Jesus' blood that provides our purity and cleansing. Because of his sacrifice, we have been made whole and new:

> *Ephesians 5:25-27 NIV[9]*
> *25 Husbands, love your wives, just as Christ loved the church and gave himself up for her 26 to make her holy, cleansing her by the washing with water through the word, 27 and to present her to himself as a radiant church, without stain or wrinkle or any other blemish, but holy and blameless.*

Blood is what seals a covenant, both in Old Testament times and in the New. In the Old Covenant, it was the blood of a sacrificial animal to pay for redemption. In the New Testament, it was Jesus' blood that paid for our redemption. It is only through the blood of our Savior that we can have wholeness in our marriages. Jesus gave everything, even to his very last drop of blood, to ransom us from the bonds of sin and death. Have you laid down your life to this extent in your own marriage?

A wedding is not meant to be just a great party. It is a memorial stone in which we can look back and remember the solemnity of the promises we made. In our marriages, we are meant to be a representation of the intimacy and closeness God desires with His people. But how can we be that representation when there is disjointedness, disunity, and a refusal to commit wholeheartedly to one another? So many people think that marriage is going to bog them down, that they will lose their freedom and their individual identity. And to a certain extent, that is absolutely what should happen. Just like the shattering of the glass is meant to signify that one's old life of singleness is over, so our marriages create a new identity. We become one new person, a new creation as husband and wife. This should also sound familiar, in that, as we are joined to Christ spiritually, we become a new creation—after His likeness and righteousness. What an honor it is to partner with the Lord in walking out this most sacred and beautiful relationship example.

# MARRIAGE ACTIVATION 7

The power of a covenant is only realized when we lay down our lives to become united with our spouse. We must leave behind our wants and desires, and look forward to all that God has for us in this miracle of marriage. To know that we get to represent the mystery of relationship with Jesus through our healthy marriages is a profound honor and responsibility.

1. Do you think you have shattered the glass, so to speak? Have you left behind your life of singleness to be wholly devoted to your spouse? If not, what are things you are holding on to from your past that are causing disunity, and resentment within your relationship?

**Marriage Activity:** Take some time to pray together and ask the Lord to help you leave behind anything that has kept a wall between you and your spouse.

Even though what has been discussed in this chapter is Jewish symbolism, it will revolutionize your life. Get a glass and wrap it up in a prayer cloth. Both of you pray over and anoint the prayer cloth with oil. Take it to a hard surface in your house, and both of you stomp on it together. Then repent verbally to one another those things that you feel have created separations between you and then privately renew your vow to be devoted to each other and the Lord from this day forward which will further strengthen your marriage covenant.

# CHAPTER 8

## SOMETIMES IT'S THE LITTLE THINGS

Anyone who has tried to light a fire in a wood stove knows that if you only put big pieces of wood in first, the fire is never going to light. That's because every good fire starts with kindling—the small stuff. It's the small stuff that causes the fire to light and continue burning. This is also the same for your marriage. It won't be the big things that keep the love, passion, and closeness going in your relationship, but the little things that you do together consistently over the long haul that keep those marriage embers ablaze.

What are some examples of kindling you can add to your fire to reignite your marriage flame?

- Date night once a week
- Post-it love notes on the refrigerator or mirror
- Sexy private texts to purposefully be flirtatious
- A touch or a pat throughout the evening in the home.

- Sending your song back and forth to each other at different times
- Dancing in the kitchen
- A good old-fashioned water fight, to bring back the fun
- Something spontaneous that you used to do that you know your spouse would remember and enjoy

Sometimes, it's the little things that matter the most. We are often so concerned with the big things that the little ones can slip through our defenses and start causing havoc.

**Catch the "Foxes"**

> *Song of Songs 2:15 NIV*[32]
> *15 Catch for us the foxes,*
> *the little foxes*
> *that ruin the vineyards,*
> *our vineyards that are in bloom.*

You might be wondering what the big deal is about little foxes? Maybe you think of a classic Disney cartoon about a fox and a hound dog that become unlikely friends? Foxes are cute, right? Foxes are indeed small, but they are not *cute*. They were detrimental to vineyards in biblical times. Because they could not reach the grapes so high up on the trellises, they would chew through the bottom branches instead. When they had chewed through the whole supporting branch, the vines that were up off the ground would fall down, and the foxes could get at the grapes. They wouldn't just steal a few grapes. They would destroy whole sections of the vine. Thus, even *little* foxes had to be eradicated from vineyards. The vinedressers had to flush them out and destroy them in order to save their crop and prevent irreparable damage to their vines.

Marital foxes are not cute. The little compromises we make in our hearts can have deadly consequences. For example, as you began your marriage, you seemed to talk all the time. It didn't even have to be about anything in particular, right? What were the things you talked about the most before you were married and while you were engaged? *Life. Dreams.* What made you laugh? Memories from your childhood. Anything and *everything* that you could talk about that told your future spouse who you really were. Why is it that, after we get married, we stop trying to discover and explore new things about the person we love the most?

Where did the little things go after you were married? Well, life happened. You start having to *adult*: paying bills, having children, and all the sleepless nights that come with them, juggling schedules. You keep on with the daily grind, until the only time you seem to talk about anything is when there is a problem. You slip into survival mode or business mode. You have stopped being partners in a covenant of marriage and you've started becoming negotiators in the operation of a home.

When was the last time you and your spouse took time

to ask meaningful questions of one another to try to rekindle your love? When did you try to find something out about them that you never knew before? When was the last time you took a moment to remember what brings your spouse joy, and then did it for them? Why do we stop doing the little things we know we *can do* that bring such joy and significance to the one we devoted our entire life to fulfilling?

What if you spent time diving into deeper conversations that help you both explore your dreams, desires, or the challenges you are facing? The problem with the little things, even the good things, is that they often get overlooked because of laziness and simply being selfish. You stopped learning about each other because you felt that wasn't a necessity going forward in your relationship. However, the little things are the bedrock of what created the relationship in the first place. You stopped taking the time to really *see* each other. That's what intimacy is: *into me, you see*. I allow you to see the deepest parts of my soul that make me who I am, and vice versa. When a couple can have a loving and continually intimate connection like that, it is a true treasure.

So how do you develop a love like that? The key is to make it a priority. Truthfully, every couple has to be intentional about this to make it happen. Yes, I said it: *priority*. We allow our busy lives to steal all our free time away from us, and then we end up emotionally bankrupt and distant from our spouse. If you can take an hour or more for television viewing each night, but you don't have time for more than a ten-minute conversation with your spouse, something is horribly wrong. What if you replaced that hour of

TV watching with an hour of conversation with your spouse, bringing back the little things and making your relationship the priority? How would it change your marriage? How would it increase your intimacy with one another? The key is to give each other the space needed to reconnect emotionally and physically.

---

Staring back at me from the bathroom floor is a pile of dirty clothes. Specifically, size-large gym shorts, one sweaty workout shirt, well-worn briefs, haphazardly balled-up socks, and a hunting hat that probably could have used a funeral a long time ago. As usual, the mass of neglected garments sits, not *inside,* but *beside* our hamper, clear evidence that my husband has been on the scene. Once again, he has neglected his one and only task I asked of him to complete the laundry process for me. *Put the clothes in the hamper!*

Today, as I look back at the messy mound, I fold my arms across my chest, and a big smile crosses my face. I laugh, even. I catch myself elbowing past annoyance and choosing gratitude instead.

I once heard a radio talk-show host doling out advice to a very contentious and frustrated bride who had called to tattle on her clutter-hound of a husband. "It sounds to me like you've got two options," the radio talk host said. "You can live in happiness with a sometimes-frustrating husband, or you can live in sparkling cleanliness all alone." The comment went deep, both for the caller and for me.

Despite occasional bow equipment or hunting paraphernalia in the kitchen, spare sunflower seeds dotting the floorboard of our car, unwashed dishes left stacked on his bedside table, and derelict duds strewn everywhere about our house, I thank my Heavenly Father. I thank Him for giving me a man to know and be known by, to love and be loved by, to serve and to be served by every day. Laughter fills this home, instead of silent OCD cleaning. Water fights and the sound of my husband's footsteps pounding across the floor as he chases our children and scoops them up in his arms is the symphony I get to listen to. I love it dearly and wouldn't change a thing about it.

Honestly, I still have to get reminders like the one I heard on the radio. I have to remind myself to calm down and enjoy those little things, because that is what life is made of. That is what makes life so unspeakably beautiful. Those tiny little things that bring us reminders, even annoying ones, that we have someone to love for the rest of our lives.

I now like to think of our usually messy home as not just a mess, but *lived-in*. My darling husband may be prone to untidiness, but untidy companionship carries a certain appeal when it involves such a magnificent human being. He has taught me to let my hair down and enjoy the little moments. There will always be laundry to do and dishes to get cleaned, but our children will not always be this small and scampering around our home. And I'd rather spend my life on them rather than stressing over a house that looks like a tornado ran through it. What a wonderful tornado he is (and our two children, who are just like him). I wouldn't have it any other way. This is what I call a life fulfilled.

— NICOLE BOYD

# MARRIAGE ACTIVATION 8

The littlest gestures can have the most profound impact. They not only show that you care about your spouse during important moments. Most often, love is shown through the day-to-day, mundane tasks and activities. Your spouse not only wants your heart and thoughts on rare occasions, but throughout your life, in every situation that knits you together.

1. Make a quick list of the little things that your spouse does that causes you to remember them throughout the day, even the annoying ones, (like clothes not put in the hamper.)

2. Come up with three meaningful questions for your spouse. And not just surface-level questions. Think about questions you might have asked when you were dating, when you couldn't seem to get enough time with them. Prepare those questions and be ready to have some fun with your spouse later this evening. (Text them so they can be prepared with their questions so they don't feel left out if they haven't been reading this chapter with you.)
3. What are the little foxes that have been chewing through the vines of your marriage? Write them down and save them to discuss at a later time.

Here's the next fun activity. Set aside a good chunk of time, turn off all distractions, and both of you pick one little thing you used to do for each other and secretly do that this week.

# PART 3
## COMMUNICATION

*"We're often afraid of being vulnerable,
but vulnerability creates genuine connection."
— Gabby Bernstein*

# CHAPTER 9

## COMMUNICATION LOST

Many couples are searching for a solution to their communication problem within their marriages. It may be safe to say that the single biggest problem of communication is that some people's actions speak so loudly that others cannot hear what they are trying to say. Someone can tell you that they love you, but it doesn't necessarily mean they do, unless it's backed up with actions that support their statements. Communication has to be supported, not just by what is discussed or talked about, but by the actions of sacrifice and servanthood that are present within a marriage. Here are a few Biblical guidelines for learning what you can do to minimize the negative actions that hinder communication within your marriage.

1. **Communication isn't just with words.**

Be aware of the messages you are sending your spouse

with your facial gestures, tone, or body language that do not communicate love. Paul writes in *I Corinthians 13:1-2 NIV*[33]:

> *"If I speak in the tongues of men and of angels, but have not love, I am only a resounding gong or a clanging cymbal. If I have the gift of prophecy and can fathom all mysteries and all knowledge, and if I have a faith that can move mountains, but have not love, I am nothing."*

We are not only responsible for what we intend to communicate, but how others understand the messages we convey through nonverbal communication. This is very problematic in many marriages. Communication becomes so platonic and systematic that the only way of knowing the emotion behind what's being said is by the nonverbal gestures presented within it. Those nonverbal ways of communication are usually the beginning of an erosion in healthy communication within marriages. The problem is, this person has started going through the motions to appease their spouse. They do this to avoid conflict while still trying to convey how they really feel, which becomes a vent valve for their pent-up frustrations and resentments.

---

> Because I am not a confrontational person, nonverbal cues can become a very bad habit for me. I am an internal processor. I need time to untangle what I'm feeling and thinking so I can present it in the right way. However, my feelings are still glaringly

apparent in facial gestures. I was once told I have very loud eyes. My husband, on the other hand, is very much a verbal processor. He has to speak it out loud to get his thoughts and feelings in order, and sometimes the things that come flying out of his mouth can seem insensitive.

When my husband and I first got married, I tended to give a lot of signs of how I was feeling with nonverbal communication. These could include banging cupboards, sighing loudly while I run the vacuum, or muttering under my breath. My husband calls this rage cleaning. He comes from a very loud and boisterous family, and they often work out their differences all together in a very loud manner, which is fine. But I grew up very differently. We were a loud family when we were having fun, but not when there was disagreement. I honestly don't think I ever saw my parents fight one time in front of us. I know they did this to protect us and present a united front. But I sometimes wish we had seen them fight, so I could have seen how a healthy confrontation was to be conducted. When my husband and I got married, there were a lot of fights we had where I would simply shut down because of the tone he used to convey his feelings. I interpreted his loudness as he was angry with me, and my go-to response was to turn inward and protect myself.

Over the years, after many drag-out fights, I have learned that it's not unChristlike to voice how I'm really feeling, even in a heated way. Burying what I was feeling and using passive-aggressive ways to express myself were not a healthy means of communication. Now I have come to realize that loud does not always equal *angry,* but passionate. And my husband has also learned where I could be misinterpreting the signals he is conveying with his tone. Always be mindful of what your spouse is trying to convey, and learn to come to a middle ground. He has learned to be more gentle and tender with his tone, and I have learned to be bolder in trying to communicate what I am truly feeling and thinking.

— NICOLE BOYD

---

### 2. Marriage communication must be *consistent*.

You can't communicate something one day, one way, and then totally change that on another day and expect your spouse to understand what you meant or need. Marriages that lack consistency in their communication are headed for disaster very soon. Jesus said, *"You will know them by their fruits."* (Matt. 7:16) If you are lacking fruit in your communication, this could be because of inconsistent communication practices. When communication breaks down between a husband and a wife, Satan is always waiting in the wings. Then, what often takes place are power struggles, the silent treatment, or deception. Many of the larger problems in marriage stem from poorly navigated conversations. How many hours, or minutes, did you spend this week engaged in conversation or activity with your spouse that did not revolve around working on the family budget, talking about the children, or watching TV? You stopped making time for your spouse, letting the children come before the marriage relationship, or from a fear of conflict. Good conversations will involve a positive exchange that is consistent, allowing for growth in a relationship. You will always be competing against your sinful, selfish nature. You will always need to be seeking God's strength to forgive. You will often struggle to find balance between your calendars and your marriage. If you keep Christ at the center of your marriage and strive to maintain unity, you will discover the blessing of great marriage communication. This is why setting aside some time at different intervals in the week and being consistent with those conversations can be so helpful.

3. **Avoiding Negative and Toxic Communication Patterns.**

• **Stay Open.** If you want to have good communication with your spouse, there needs to be a level of openness and transparency. As you share with each other, both your thoughts and feelings, you will be able to communicate on a logical level and a soul level.

In order for openness to happen in communication, there must be a feeling of safety where you both know that you will not be judged or criticized when you honestly share from your heart and soul. Staying open requires both spouses to first, not correct or interrupt the other person. And, second, not to make jokes or bring sarcasm into the discussion. These two things will always create a shutdown to positive and open communication. Openness builds up trust as you learn to appreciate one another's strengths and protect each other's vulnerabilities.

- **Encourage and Compliment.** If you want to improve your communication skills, remember, you have the wonderful opportunity to compliment and encourage one another.

That means where one of you is weak or lacking in some way, the other can fill in, so together you make a complete and whole marriage. By working together and communicating with each other as a team, you can achieve so much more than you could as two separate individuals. That is why you encourage and compliment one another in order to avoid creating a toxic environment, which in turn, creates a shutdown in your openness and transparency. I would suggest, that every time you communicate with your spouse that you have multiple moments and strategic impartations of encouragement.

- **Use Physical Touch (NOT Sexual Touch).** Touch, such as holding hands and sitting together closely, can break down the barrier of distance that the enemy loves to create in marriage communication. You will have to fight for this because usually setting aside time for communication comes with some intense feelings and moments of heated expression. This is why physical touch in this process is so important. It creates a bond that can never be broken as you communicate the difficult or strategic things. Physical touch may not happen every time because it may not be conducive to where you are at that moment. But whenever you can instigate this, it will create an instant connection that will assist in your healthy communication process.

4. **Don't assume that your spouse can read your mind.**

In Ephesians 4:15, Paul exhorts us to *speak the truth in love*, not read your partner's mind. You may be able to anticipate what your spouse wants or needs as you spend life with them. Do not assume that they can read your mind and know what you are thinking and feeling at all times. This is not only impractical but incredibly unfair to your spouse. Healthy communication takes voicing your feelings and thoughts in a way they can understand. This takes work and time to get good at because you and your spouse are invariably different. You have different ways of thinking and responding. You approach and handle situations differently. You have differing ways of taking information into your mind and processing that information. It is imperative that you state your position in a fresh way to make sure your spouse understands. This is always a healthy communication practice.

---

> This was a difficulty my husband and I had early on in our marriage. He thought that I would be able to read his mind and anticipate his every move. But I am, in fact, not Wonder Woman. It caused a great deal of strife for us in those first few years of marriage. But over time, we have been able to (mostly) overcome this hurdle and can realize when we are holding an unfair expectation over one another. We've come to understand that the other may not know what the other is thinking, needing, or feeling

at every given moment. Just like the adage we often use for children, communication means you have to *use your words.*

— NICOLE BOYD

---

Unfortunately, when communication breaks down between a couple, intimacy follows shortly after.

**Change the Way You Think**

> "If you think you *can*, you're right.
> If you think you *can't*, you're right."
> —Henry Ford

It all comes down to perspective. The way you think shapes your world. Your actions always follow your thoughts. If you have a negative outlook, then you will experience negative outcomes. If you do the opposite, you will experience positive outcomes in your marriage and your communication.

If you want to experience a miracle in the communication of your marriage, revert back to the way you used to act when you first fell in love, and you'll fall in love all over again. Start talking and loving each other like you used to. When you choose to re-express the love you have for one another, it grows your capacity for more love. It's so true that what you sow, you reap. If you choose to live in the light of this one concept—life without regrets—then your marriage will take on a whole new, beautiful intensity and intentionality. The bedrock for that strong foundation in marriage is communication, which is the art and technique of using words with grace to effectively impart your ideas. Following are tips for men and women in having great communication.

**Tips for Women in Communication**

- **Don't Overshare.**

The reality is, more words don't necessarily mean better communication. *Specific words* delivered with a loving atmosphere and heart create the best communication. Let's face it, ladies. Your man is probably not the big talker in the relationship. If he is the talker and you tend to be the listener, just turn this around. If your man isn't sharing as much as you think he should, it's probably because he's reached his limit of communication for the day. Men seem to bore more easily and faster than women do when it comes to talking. When you're trying to have a deep conversation, be sensitive to the signs that he's growing restless, tuning out, and trying to find a way to exit the room. The worst thing you can do in a relationship is forget how to relate to your spouse, relapse into silence, or roommate syndrome. None of these are going to build healthy and strong communication habits, and the problem usually stems from the communication being too long and unspecific, logical, or intentional.

- **Make the Experience Enjoyable and Pleasant**

If you make the experience pleasant for your husband, he will be more apt to focus on what you're trying to say, even though he's not looking in your eyes. Don't make it feel as if the end goal is having a conversation so you can feel good about yourself and solely what you were trying to communicate. The goal is intimacy, and in order for there to be intimacy, there needs to be vulnerability. Refer back to the first sentence. It is harder for men to be vulnerable, especially in a culture where it is often said that men need to be the strong ones. Statements such as these are prevalent: men don't cry, men are not supposed to feel, and so on. Be patient with him and allow him the time and space he needs to meet you in that intimate place of deep communication. And be sure that he knows that anything that is said between you will be held in the strictest of confidence. The worst thing that can happen is that you will use something he has shared in vulnerability against him later, or share it with someone outside the marriage. This will not make communication enjoyable or pleasant, and you will reap what you have sown the next time you really want to talk to him, (regardless of how much clothing you have removed.)

- **Communicate Your Genuine Interest**

The goal is to get to know one another better, right? Wives, communicate your genuine interest in getting to know him better—not for who you *think* he is or *want* him to be, but for who he truly is. You married him for *him*.

What is it that made him attractive to you? Press into getting to know him better in every season of his life. Throughout your marriage together, your communication process will evolve. Not only because you have history together, but because you have created patterns and practices with how you communicate. This can be a good thing or a bad thing. He doesn't want to feel like he's just another item on your to-do list, and that's the only reason you ever want to talk to him. Through my thirty years of counseling, I have discovered that men change subtly, but drastically, as they live life. It is important to recognize that your communication will have to change and grow as well.

If you follow these steps, you will see that it is easy for your man to open up to you. It takes a lot of trust, patience, and practice to get good at communication. But the rewards are forever life-changing for both of you.

## Tips for Men in Communication

- **Communication Involves Talking.**

This may sound rudimentary, but somehow, many men have forgotten this key ingredient. You cannot have positive and healthy marriage communication if you're not using words. One of the most attractive things for your wife can be when you initiate a healthy conversation. Remember, you are different from her. She might not want to see all that stuff (wink, wink) while you're trying to talk sincerely to her. (Or maybe she does.) Even so, she wants to feel that you're actually going to listen if you initiate a conversation.

You're not just trying to have the conversation so it can lead to sex.

With all that being settled, it's very important that you don't make it superficial or awkward in your initiation of it. It needs to be planned, but it also needs to be organic in how it's facilitated. For example, write out some discussion starters in your notes on your phone while you're at work. The next time you're on a walk, on a date night, or just driving, look back and remember one of them and use that to start a conversation that she would love to participate in. Below are some examples to get you started.

**Communication Starter Examples:**

- If you could go listen to your favorite band/musician, who would that be and why?
- What was your favorite subject in school? Who was your favorite teacher?
- If you could travel anywhere in the world, where would you like to go?
- What do you see us doing together after the kids have left the house and we are empty nesters?
- What would you like us to start planning in preparation for retirement?

- **You Don't Need to Fix Everything.** Remember, you probably don't have to fix anything, even though you're going to think you do. As men, because we are mostly involved in problem-solving in our vocations, we have a tendency to look at all of our conversations through this lens. This can be very destructive in your marriage. Much of communication is the expression of feelings, ideas, and desires. She doesn't need you to fix anything. She just wants you to care about what she cares about.

- **Communication Never Involves Multitasking.** This is important, men. Even though you may have the gift of doing multiple things at once, your wife will *never* feel like this is an appropriate communication strategy while she is trying to talk to you. Communication is focused and attentive in its process, meaning it needs undivided attention at all times. This is so important for your spouse. She needs to know that what she is trying to say to you is getting through. She wants to know you're paying attention to her, you're understanding where she is coming from, and that you really care. All too often, men are working or doing something else when they are communicating with a colleague. That's just how your day goes. Your wife, however, sees this as you not being considerate and understanding. *Stop* and be present with whatever she's trying to share with you at that moment. She really needs you to hear her.

There is a very helpful book called *The Five Languages of Love* by Gary Chapman. I'm sure you've heard of it. As a part of your homework for this lesson, I'd like you to get a copy to read together. If you've already read it, read it again. It is vital to know what "fills your partner's love tank." It is important to know this about your wife, because you experience love a certain way, and nine times out of ten, your way differs from your spouse's way.

For example, you may feel most loved when your wife makes lunch for you, or when she makes sure your laundry is done. So, your natural response is to do things for her, right? But that's not filling her "love tank." She may feel most loved when you sit down and listen to her talk about her day. Often couples speak different languages. You might be on totally different wavelengths, so to speak. It takes time, patience, and humility to learn to speak another language, right? And it's going to take time to learn how to communicate your love for your spouse in their "native language." The following are the five love languages detailed in Chapman's book:

1. *Words of Affirmation (verbal encouragement)*
2. *Quality time*
3. *Gifts*
4. *Acts of service*
5. *Touch (physical and/or sexual)*

What happens when two people have different views and needs? Often, conflict arises. Does this mean that if you and your partner have different love languages or ways of doing and thinking about things, you are destined to divorce? Absolutely not! There is going to be conflict in a marriage. There is just no way around that. Conflict simply means that there is a tension between you, and there needs to be a way for you to come to a middle ground. This cannot be altered without you understanding your spouse, and your spouse understanding you through healthy communication. Conflict is an opportunity for you to show love to your spouse by trying to walk in their shoes and see things from a different perspective. It is a chance to lay down your wants and desires for the good of what *they* want and need in that moment, instead of what you want and need. Because our society has created a Me Culture, we have a tendency to write ourselves into every narrative being communicated. That is seldom healthy.

With conflict, there is not just the visible conflict arising, but a simultaneous battle in the mind, spirit, and soul. People are different. I know, it's a no-brainer. But when people get into a marriage, they somehow expect their spouse to be able to read their minds. That in itself is going to cause a lot of conflict. Here are some common differences between men and women that have been listed by different resources.

- **The top 5 needs for men:**

  1. *Sexual Fulfillment*
  2. *Recreational Companionship*
  3. *Attractive Appearance*
  4. *Domestic Support*
  5. *Respect and Admiration*

- **The top 5 needs for women:**

  1. *Conversation*
  2. *Honesty & Openness*
  3. *Financial Support*
  4. *Family Commitment*
  5. *Affection*

You can see how different the needs are depending on whether you're a man or a woman. If you look at these lists, what's at the top for a man is most likely at the bottom for a woman. There is nothing wrong with that. Instead of trying to change each other, why don't we celebrate these differences?

It's not enough to just celebrate them. We need to try to fulfill the needs of our spouse as best we can. This was made obvious by the lists above and what was said earlier in this paragraph. Men, you're going to need to be open to conversation before sexual fulfillment, and ladies, if you want conversation, you're going to need to instigate sexual fulfillment. That's just how it works. Quit fighting it, and make your marriage great by understanding and making room for each other's differences. There will be a lot less friction, frustration, and resentment if couples would learn this secret ingredient that will cause their communication to truly be enriched and grow.

Once again, this comes down to humility, sacrifice, and the biblical principle of putting the other person above yourself. It takes thinking of your spouse before yourself. It takes laying down your life.

Period.

That's what makes a marriage *great*.

# MARRIAGE ACTIVATION 9

This week, focus on really analyzing your communication process within your marriage and finding potential struggles. Then, answer the following:

1. Good communication is important to me because: _____
2. What are the areas you discovered as a couple throughout this chapter that will help increase healthy communication in your relationship in the future?
3. Make a wish list of 3 things you want your spouse to do more often when it comes to communication:

Now, block out a section of time, pull out the lists you made with the answers to the above questions, and read them out loud to one another, one at a time. Take your time on them. Don't try to get through all of them just so you can say you finished the activation. That's not the point. The point is to use the proper communication you learned from this chapter to discuss these areas of challenge within your relationship.

**Prayer:**

Take a few moments after you've done this activity and pray about areas that you feel have restricted and divided proper communication. It is very important that you bring them before the Lord as an act of repentance. Do so individually and take responsibility for what you have done to cause barriers and walls in your marriage communication. You're not praying for how to fix the other person, you're confessing before your spouse how you have contributed to improper communication as a petition and request of change before the Lord.

# CHAPTER 10

## I JUST WANT TO BE FRIENDS AGAIN

Whenever a couple who is going through a really rough time requests counseling with me and I can sense there is a major separation between them in the spirit, I start our counseling session with this one powerful question. "When did you get a divorce?"

Obviously, they respond that they have not legally divorced yet. But a divorce doesn't happen on paper first. It happens in the heart and in the physical and spiritual realm, way before it ever goes to a courtroom. This is always a shock and eye-opener to the couple. They usually start to defend themselves by stating, "That's why we're coming to counseling. We don't want a divorce." The reason I do this is to show them that if they don't change their hearts and spirits towards one another immediately, the paperwork is just semantics. I use this question to open their eyes. They have likely begun the separation process from each other before the legal divorce paperwork has ever been filed.

When a couple in this situation comes in for counseling, I have them take out a piece of paper and write down the answers to these questions: "When did you stop being best friends and start being roommates with occasional conjugal visits? When did you stop enjoying the physical touch of your lover? When did you stop enjoying spending time with one another?" The purpose for this directness is to help the couple pinpoint where they became emotionally and spiritually divided.

If you find yourselves in this place, I want to be very clear that there is hope. Your marriage doesn't have to stay this way. We are going to dive deeper into what it takes to rekindle the friendship you once enjoyed, how to build upon that, and make it even stronger. First, there are some subtle, yet detrimental, roadblocks that can sneak in and cause a breakdown in your marital friendship:

1. **You Stopped Caring About What Your Spouse Cares About**

Have you stopped watching the sports event your spouse loves (and you claimed to love) when you were dating? Did you stop taking romantic walks and holding hands like you did when you were dating? Did you stop making out and kissing like you did when you were dating? Did you stop being flirty and fun like you were when you were dating? This is very important. Before we go any further with this chapter, you need to add one specific entry to this list and say it out loud to your spouse. What is it that you miss that you used to do together before you got married?

This goes back to the Defraudment Clause. This is one of the biggest conflicts that begins to build bitterness toward your spouse. Whether you did it consciously or not, by not continuing to do those things you enjoyed from before you were married, it communicates that you only did those things to get your spouse's commitment. It seems that you were lying the whole time about wanting to do that thing that was so special to them, essentially to entrap them. What are those things that you need to go back and reinstate into your marriage that have gotten lost because of time or laziness?

2. **You Choose To Hold Onto That Grudge**

The loss of friendship in a marriage is often the result of all the disappointments that arise from promises not being fulfilled. Because of this, resentments and grudges are held as an emotional protective mechanism against being hurt in the future. It is painful to hold onto a belief that our spouse will follow through with what they say when the evidence proves otherwise. This is extremely detrimental to the future of a marriage, and especially, a friendship. No one wants to be disappointed over and over again by somebody who claims to have good intentions with no evidence of that love being produced. Over time, a grudge replaces all those false promises with sarcasm, guilt, and silence.

There has to be a moment where we admit to our spouse that we are holding a grudge from unmet promises that are stopping our friendship and love from growing. This is an extremely vulnerable moment because the likelihood is, these exact things have been discussed millions of times before. Because of this, the friendship grows weaker while the grudges grow stronger. However, this is not an excuse to continue this pattern. Something has to change in order for your friendship to be restored. Either you have to change your expectations of the unmet promises that are possibly never going to be fulfilled, or you must let your spouse know what they are doing and how it affects you. This is important in order to protect our friendship and the integrity of our marriage covenant. This is what really defines a great marriage from a platonic marriage. Friendship has to be present in order for the marriage to be a great one. There are no other options.

### 3. You Stopped Being Companions and Started Being Business Partners

The whole reason that you fell in love in the first place was because you thought this person was compatible with you and wanted to be your companion. Companionship with your spouse is the healing balm to every situation and circumstance that could ever arise. The problem is, companionship starts to erode when people start pursuing their own interests separate from their spouses. Companionship means that two people have shared common experiences that led to shared feelings and rewarding outcomes. If the only time you have fun is when you're not around your spouse, how in the world will you ever have a friendship together and maintain any form of closeness or companionship?

Some of you may have the excuse that you don't have

common interests or that God made you different. I bet if you were to make it a matter of prayer, God would reveal something to you that you could both begin to enjoy together. Take a few minutes now to discuss some ideas of what those things may be.

Unfortunately, many relationships get the intimacy out of order. A couple begins with sexual intimacy, but doesn't cultivate emotional intimacy first. Because of this, the soul tie that is created from the sexual union creates a false sense of friendship and companionship. This is later revealed within the marriage because at one point the two individuals will look at one another and have nothing to do or nothing in common but sex. If you've gotten intimacy out of order, you have to face the reality that your relationship was built on physical intimacy instead of emotional intimacy. Emotional intimacy is companionship and friendship. You've created major complications that you are now going to have to rectify in order to have a viable and strong marriage. It doesn't take a couple very long to realize that the sexual aspect can never be the long term foundation of that relationship or marriage.

True friendship is what holds a marriage together through the ups and downs, the conflicts and trials. For your friendship to continue and grow, there must be mutual respect for each other. Time is so important, as it is the only commodity that we can give that truly costs us something. It is the most precious thing we can give, for we only have a finite amount of time on this earth. Money is easy to come by, but it is a cheap stand-in for our time and attention. If more possessions or money were the key to marital bliss, gold-diggers would be among the happiest people on earth—but they are not.

Friendship is what makes a marriage strong and worthwhile. When all else fails, when beauty fades, possessions break, or all you have left is the shirt on your back, can you still say you are rich because of your spouse's friendship? Here are some examples of what real friends do.

- They talk and share about vulnerable things nobody else will ever know.
- They confide secrets in each other.
- They make it a practice to learn more about each other.
- They keep their friendship consistent and alive by spending quality time discussing dreams, ideas, and goals with each other.

Spending one's life on another, laying down our own wants for the sake of our best friend, and working together toward a common goal—this is real, lasting friendship.

# MARRIAGE ACTIVATION 10

Companionship and friendship is what makes a marriage worthwhile. Throughout the next week, take stock of how your marriage is doing in the area of friendship.

1. How close are you to your spouse? Rate it on a scale of 1 to 10. Both of you do that now, privately and quietly. Then compare before going any further.
2. It's amazing to me how many guys say '8' and their wife says '2'. The only way to become closer friends is to do it on purpose. Left alone without a goal, married people drift apart. That's why the numbers are off. One is not realizing how the other is not being fulfilled. Marriages don't fall apart, they drift apart. Here is an example of lack of fulfillment from the

Dear Abby column. Put yourself in this couple's shoes as you read:

*DEAR ABBY, I am a 42-year-old man with three wonderful children. They are all grown and in their 20s. (Yes, we had them young.) I have been married for 23 years and things have been good between my wife and me.*

*About a year ago, my wife—who is an accountant—decided she wanted to try real estate. She took a class, got her license, and now sells real estate part time. She's doing so well at it that she plans on quitting her accounting job soon and concentrating on real estate full time.*

*My problem is I have been having empty nest syndrome, and now my wife is working every weekend. On week nights, I sit and watch TV by myself while she works away on her computer. On the weekends I try to keep busy doing jobs around the house and cleaning, but I'm bored, lonely and depressed. I have mentioned this to my wife; she says I should find a hobby.*

*Abby, I don't want a hobby. I want to be with my wife. She absolutely loves her new job and talks about it constantly. I don't want to ask her to quit her job, because she would resent me for it. (And no, I don't want to sell real estate with her.) Any suggestions? — MISERABLE IN MICHIGAN*

3. Imagine for a moment you've become the counselor. Both of you discuss how you would counsel this gentleman from the *Dear Abby*

column through his conflict with his wife's newfound vocation. Plan on taking some time on this. You may need to pause here for a few days or a week before you start the next chapter. It is amazing to me how many marriages have this exact problem in some way, and don't want to admit it. They wonder why they've lost the ability to be best friends.

# CHAPTER 11

## BECOMING FAITHFUL STEWARDS IN YOUR FINANCES

### BY JIM WEAVER

It is not uncommon to discover that one of the sources of strife in a marriage is arguments about money. In fact, money fights are often one of the top-stated reasons for divorce. Yes, this can be rooted in the lack of money or disagreements in how a couple's money is spent. But truth be told, there are usually a few core reasons why fights about money are so prevalent. Usually, these issues are rooted in misaligned values and poor communication.

It is easy to blame money itself. Statements such as "Money is evil," or "If we only had more money," are often excuses of why there are fights and divisions. But these statements are only symptoms of the greater problem. The money situation a couple finds themselves in is often the result of the values they hold in the area of money. How is it possible to see one couple with very little to their name in complete unity and joy, while another couple with an abundance of income is in tremendous strife? It's because the money situation is only the fruit of the shared, misaligned values of the couple.

First of all, we must establish that money is neither evil nor good. Money just *is*. Money is a tool of commerce that we employ in order to purchase the items we need or want. The outcome of its flow is dependent on the way it is used. Money has a current. It has a flow. This is why it is called currency. It moves from one place to another based on the job it is given to do. Even the fact that some people have an abundance of money and others don't is not a moral or emotional construct. Money can be used to do good or to do evil. Its trajectory is sourced in *people* who *decide* what it will do. So to blame money itself for our problems is shortsighted. As a married couple, your fights about money have a deeper root than the mere lack or abundance of money.

Before you can achieve victory in your marriage in the area of finances, you must view finances from a biblical standpoint. It might be surprising to hear that you have been arguing and divided over the use of something that doesn't belong to you in the first place. Biblically speaking, humans are merely stewards of God's resources. We don't actually own any of it. We simply manage it for God as our act of submission and trust.

*Psalm 24:1 NKJV*[34]
*The earth is the Lord's, and all its fullness,*
*The world and those who dwell therein.*

Before you can walk forward in unity in your marriage in the use of finances, you must acknowledge that money is not something you own—it is something you steward.

## You Are Simply A Steward

Stewardship is the careful and responsible use or management of something that has been entrusted to your care. The way we handle the money we have reveals the character of our hearts, the quality of our relationships, and the level of trust in God. Every breath you breathe, every skill you possess that helps you receive an income, and every creative idea you come up with that results in financial advancement, comes from God. If it weren't for Him and His blessing, you wouldn't have anything at all. Everything we have is something God has allowed us to have in order to take care of it. If we can pry our figurative fingers off of our income, we can begin the process of healing and stewarding what God has allowed us to use. Then we can begin to align with our spouse as to how we use the finances we have access to.

Money is a great revealer. Is there greed or fear in your heart? Money and how you spend it will reveal those things that otherwise might have remained hidden. Are you generous with your finances, as God asks us to be, or are you tight-fisted when it comes to helping others? Pressure reveals the intentions of our hearts. We may say that we are generous, but when pressure comes, such as not being able to afford groceries one week, our true character is showcased for all to see. Will we continue to be faithful in our tithes, or will we cave under the pressure and try to wrest control of our provision from God's hands?

God owns it all. This should cause us to evaluate how we are using God's resources. Using the biblical definition that we are merely stewards of God's resources, how would you rate your use of what belongs to Him? Do you make sure that God is on the top line of your budget by giving tithes and offerings before you pay yourself for anything else? If God is on top, you'll never miss giving to Him. If He's not, you'll pay yourself first, which often means you'll begin to live outside of your means. In our Western culture, we justify large amounts of consumer debt, mortgages, extravagant vacations, and lavish lifestyles, all while complaining about inflation and needing a raise. What if we started by giving God His ten percent, staying out of debt, and taking care of the most important things in our lives and families before we take care of our own personal wants or entertainment? When God is first, and a large portion of your paycheck stays in your bank account instead of being sent to a creditor to pay for yesterday, you'll find you have a lot less stress and a whole lot more vision for your future. Now imagine you and your spouse on the same page with finances, a buffer of money, an emergency fund saved, a generous heart that keeps God and others first, and *no debt* whatsoever. Sounds nice, doesn't it? This is God's desire for you and your spouse.

Whether we acknowledge that what we have comes from God or not, it's apparent that the abundance or lack of money can play a significant role in the health of our marriages. If there is no lack and there is peace in your relationship, most other things seem to align as well. When there is strife, disagreement, dishonesty, or entitlement in the area of personal finances, the marriage is strained and the vision for the future is hamstrung. This is a big deal. Come into unity regarding money, and many other things will line up on their own.

## You Are Different Than Your Spouse On Purpose

Most likely, you and your spouse see money completely differently. One of you is a spender. Shopping seems like a spiritual gift, and giving over money in exchange for a good deal is entertainment. On the other hand, one of you is likely a saver. The thought of parting with any money at all is terrifying, and your partner's spending habits not only annoy you sometimes but can actually cause you to fear for your future. Whether your differences are subtle or extreme, these different ways of looking at money can create strain.

If you were raised in poverty, you'll likely operate in a poverty mentality, seeing money as your source of security. The absence of money may be the worst fear you can imagine. If you were raised in abundance or with entitlement, you might use the spending of money as a way to comfort your need for entertainment or status. Either way, your origin story with money will play out in your marriage in some way. The only way to overcome your differences in how you handle money is to become intentional with vulnerable, regular communication on the subject. You must learn each other's *money language* in order to build a new and healthy purpose for your marriage. To assume you'll just figure it out is a recipe for disaster.

## My Money Vs. Your Money

When you said "I do", you committed your life to your spouse. This means not only your heart, with its love and emotions, but everything else, too. Your time was pledged.

Your faithfulness and commitment were pledged. You promised to be together in sickness and health, in good times and bad times, as long as you both shall live. If you can share a bed, you should be able to share finances. But often a couple is willing to share everything except their finances. In almost every case, the best way for a couple to operate financially is with one shared bank account. This keeps the couple away from the roommate mentality, where one person pays the rent while the other pays for groceries out of their separate paychecks. If you share your income, making it a household income, you won't need to pay each other back for your dinner out. You'll make your budget together and spend your income according to this plan out of your shared resources.

One of the most difficult things new couples will do is disclose to one another the state of their finances. The way someone stewards their finances reveals the nature of their character. And often, one or both parties may think the best thing to do is keep their finances secret. However, this is a recipe for massive resentment. In a marriage, the language should change from "me" to "we". *We* have a mortgage. *We* have a phone bill. *We* pay for electricity. *We* save for a vacation. These are *our* cars.

When couples first start out, money is often tight. And right alongside a tight budget is the pressure of culture and people around us to keep up with the Joneses. Comparison is a thief that drains bank accounts and peace in many marriages. It's also the source of most of the debt we sign up for. In a world of easy financing, it's not uncommon for a young couple to try to emulate the lifestyles of people who are many decades ahead of them financially. When other people's status is the measure of your own success, you are bound in chains before you even get started. You must determine to live within the means of your *current* income. If you've found yourself in the cyclone of trying to maintain a lifestyle you cannot afford, your first goal is to untangle yourself from your commitments. You can so this by either paying off your debt as quickly as you can or, sometimes better, sell anything and everything you can in order to eliminate debt. This creates breathing room in your budget and relationships again.

> *Proverbs 6:1-5 NKJV*[35]
> *1 My son, if you become surety for your friend,*
> *If you have shaken hands in pledge for a stranger,*
> *2 You are snared by the words of your mouth;*
> *You are taken by the words of your mouth.*
> *3 So do this, my son, and deliver yourself;*
> *For you have come into the hand of your friend:*
> *Go and humble yourself;*
> *Plead with your friend.*
> *4 Give no sleep to your eyes,*
> *Nor slumber to your eyelids.*
> *5 Deliver yourself like a gazelle from the hand of the hunter, And like a bird from the hand of the fowler.*

Entitlement and debt, along with misaligned vision and goals create stress fractures. Our financial wants and desires are not necessarily sinful. But they can be roadblocks in our relationship. If you live in such a way that the things you own, your freedom to spend, ability to travel, or how you look in the eyes of others cause you to spend beyond your means, you are at risk of shipwrecking your financial future at best. You are in danger of destroying the unity and covenant of your marriage at worst.

Money often represents different things to different people. For some, money represents security. For others, it represents status and success. If the way you and your spouse view money is different and you never reconcile these differences to create shared values, money will continue to be a fight in your marriage.

- Security

Money often represents the security and solidarity of a family unit. If there is abundance, people think they are safe. If there is a lack, people fear the worst for their future. My wife and I have discovered that peace doesn't come in the abundance of money. Peace comes in having a plan and working that plan together. This is an act of stewardship that results in an agreed-upon budget and shared direction for the future—short-term and long-term.

- Fear

Our longing for security often reveals our deepest-seated fears. Maybe your disagreements are coming from the fear that a disaster is looming right around the corner. This could be because disasters have already happened before, which makes the fear legitimate. Possibly the fear is based on an imagination that something *could* go wrong when there's no evidence it will. Or maybe the abundance of debt payments and expensive bills are triggering a fear of crisis, which is straining your marriage. It's time to have a conversation about what you value, what is making you afraid, and what you can do together to combat the fear you have around the area of money in your marriage.

- **Ambition**

Sometimes ambition can be a wedge between spouses. It's not wrong to pursue your dreams and want to see forward movement in the area of your net worth. But if ambition by one spouse or both is exacting stress on the marriage, it's time to talk about your dreams. Healthy ambition is good. Out-of-balance *ambition* will create resentment and could possibly steamroll the spouse of lesser ambition.

- **Control**

Let me ask you a question. Who controls the money in your marriage? If your answer is not that you both control the money, you might have found the source of your division. If one spouse controls the money and the other has no say at all, this is unhealthy and unbiblical. Many single-income families might argue, "But *I* make the money and he/she takes care of the house. He/she doesn't have an income, so he/she doesn't have a say." This is a recipe for a shipwreck.

*Ephesians 5:21 NKJV*[36]
*...submitting to one another in the fear of God.*

> *Ephesians 5:22 NKJV[36]*
> *Wives, submit to your own husbands...*

> *Ephesians 5:25 NKJV[36]*
> *Husbands, love your wives, just as Christ also loved the church and gave Himself for her...*

Notice submission goes both ways. Submitting to one another is where the marriage relationship *starts*. No one is to control the other. In the area of finances, your values, dreams, and ambitions are shared.

It's important for us to consider what the Bible says when thinking of our values surrounding the security of having enough money. Let's look at a few verses of scripture that can help:

> *1 Timothy 6:10 NKJV[37]*
> *For the love of money is a root of all kinds of evil, for which some have strayed from the faith in their greediness, and pierced themselves through with many sorrows.*

Notice this verse says the love of money is a root of all kinds of evil. Money itself is not evil. Our love and affection for money is a root of all kinds of evil. What this means is that if we can have money in its proper place, it makes for a great servant. We only have one Master. God never intended money to master us! It was meant to serve us as *we serve Jesus*.

*1 Timothy 6:17-19 NKJV[37]*

*17 Command those who are rich in this present age not to be haughty, nor to trust in uncertain riches but in the living God, who gives us richly all things to enjoy. 18 Let them do good, that they be rich in good works, ready to give, willing to share, 19 storing up for themselves a good foundation for the time to come, that they may lay hold on eternal life.*

- **Cooperation**

Money uncovers the character of those who possess it. What does money reveal about your personal character and the culture of your marriage? Are you a generous giver? Do you trust the Lord for your provision, or are you living in constant worry about whether you will have enough to get by? Are you happy with your honest answer? What will you do today to change and align with God's Word so your marriage can begin to thrive in the area of personal finance?

## MARRIAGE ACTIVATION 11

Money is neither good nor bad, but it does act as an agent to reveal what is in our hearts. Take some time this week to honestly answer the following questions about the state of your finances as a couple and address some areas that may need some work.

1. What are your values concerning money? I want you to take some time to write down your values separately, and then discuss them together.
2. Did you learn something you never knew about your spouse? What guides your decisions? Is it the need for security? Fear? Ambition? Are there issues that are blocking you from operating in your finances as a team?
3. What needs to shift so you can cooperate (co-operate) your finances. Do you need to give up separate checking accounts and open a joint

account? Do you need to develop a unified budget? Take the time to listen to each other so that fear and manipulation have no part in your finances.

# CHAPTER 12

## FINANCES: LET'S GET PRACTICAL

### BY JIM WEAVER

When my wife and I got married and answered the call to ministry, we understood that money could potentially be limited, as a career in proclaiming the Gospel is usually not as financially lucrative as most other professions. We started out with lots of dreams and very little money. This sacrifice was noble and honorable because we knew that if we pursued secular careers, we could probably achieve greater financial success. But we had felt God tug on our hearts and surrendered that financial dream for the dream our hearts beat for: serving God in full-time ministry and being a mouthpiece for the Gospel of Jesus Christ.

Unfortunately, in our opulent culture, we discovered that banks and other lending institutions, including credit card companies, were willing to loan us just about any amount of money we asked them for. We could *feel* financially successful even though our actual income didn't back it up. Our lifestyle could exceed our paycheck. We could *look* and *feel* wealthier than we actually were.

We decided we needed a credit card in order to build credit and in case we needed it for an emergency or travel. Next, we got a mortgage. It wasn't an excessive mortgage payment, but it was debt nonetheless. Then we financed a car. Then we started using our credit card for non-emergencies. Then we financed a trip overseas. Next, we invested in our property with some upgrades. Then we financed a pickup. Then we financed a travel trailer. Pretty soon, our monthly debt payments were as big as our income. It all worked...until it didn't. You see, with no plan, ambition that exceeded our salary, and a lack of conviction on Biblical principles in the area of money, we had painted ourselves into a corner. When we did our taxes one year, we *owed* money instead of receiving a refund. The only payment plan the IRS would authorize took the exact amount of wiggle room we had left in our very thin budget.

I say "we" in my story loosely. I've come to realize now that most of the *we* was *me*. I had all these great ideas, and my wife went along with me, thinking I knew what I was doing. We didn't discuss anything unless it was one of my whims, and she trusted me as an honoring spouse. When we had no money left over, *we* discovered that *I* had made a mess, and we were in deep trouble. Even if I wanted to, I couldn't even buy a pair of shoes for one of my toddlers in a given month. We had no savings account and no breathing room.

It was about this time that I remembered a book I had on my bookshelf. When we first married, we had picked up a book called *The Total Money Makeover* by Dave Ramsey. I had read the book and thought to myself, "This is a great plan. We should do that someday." Apparently, that day had arrived. I reached for that book again, devoured it, and we pulled together as a couple to go through the Ramsey 7 Baby Steps—a Biblical and common-sense way to steward personal finances laid out in the course *Financial Peace University*. It was the hardest thing we've ever done, but it was, aside from our salvation, one of the greatest life-changes we have ever experienced.

Though I cannot go into thorough detail in this chapter about all that we learned, I highly encourage you to go through Ramsey Solutions' *Financial Peace University* as a couple. It will transform your life. The principles I am about to lay out are based on Dave Ramsey's teaching, and you can find more at his website.*

**Admit You Have a Language Barrier**

Couples develop a language around their money ideology. If money and its use cause you and your spouse to fight, grumble, or freeze up, it's very important to dig into what the reasons might be. I'd like to describe a scenario that can demonstrate a conflict married couples tend to have around money. I'll push it to the extreme. Some couples aren't all the way to these limits, but this will demonstrate my point.

It's not uncommon in a marriage to have one spouse who is very security-minded, viewing money and its presence in the bank as an insurance policy against disasters.

---

* https://www.ramseysolutions.com/money/financial-peace

This person is often very reluctant to spend and is more prone to store things up, even if it means hardship or extreme sacrifice. While it is a noble baseline for you to have an emergency fund, this person often takes it a step further, seeing *most* spending as excessive and unnecessary. Money is seen as a way to feed the family and make sure there is a roof over their head. Today, we'll name this person Jane.

In this example, Jane is married to Greg. He works hard and plays hard. He views income as a reward for hours of sacrifice to make ends meet and sees purchases as a sign of success. If there is money in the bank account, he may view each dollar as his little friend that can make his ambitions and dreams come true. Often, the absence of dollars doesn't alarm Greg. He figures he can just make some more dollars in the future in order to pay for whatever he wants today. Whether that's a new gadget for doing yard work, a trip that will hopefully lead to a great adventure and memory, or a vehicle or piece of property that is shiny, new, and impressive, Greg doesn't like the idea of money sitting around doing nothing. Those dollars need to be spent!

Jane, on the other hand, came from a background where money was scarce. She also works hard, but does not believe that she deserves to play hard. She sees money as something that must be saved to ward off impending doom. Money is something that must be hoarded and protected because all too often, there is not enough to pay for what is needed, let alone little wants here and there. When she sees those dollars sitting safely in the account, her sense of security is increased. Conversely, when she sees them flying out of the account, it increases her anxiety that they are just one purchase away from ending up on the streets.

Maybe you see yourself on one side or the other. Of course, this is not gender-exclusive, but the scenario I painted above is not unusual. The interesting thing I want you to consider is that neither one of these money philosophies is inherently wrong if they are balanced and submitted to Christ. Remember, money is a tool. It has no morals. The *use* of money is where the morals and values of the user are revealed. The difficulty comes in the lack of communication between the spouses to agree on values, work together on goals, and appreciate the viewpoints and strengths of the other person's understanding and use of money. Greg needs Jane to hold him back from being impetuous and unwise. Jane needs Greg to help her experience a little bit of fun in life.

One person may speak the language of lack. Likely, this person grew up thinking money was so scarce that the only way to have some was to contain it somehow so it couldn't escape.

The other person may speak the language of abundance. Money is available if we work harder or figure out a slick financing option. Often this person will say things like, "You're only young once. Enjoy it while you can."

Again, variables exist. Sometimes a person who is in a lack-mentality will spend a lot on debt because they're compensating for the way they grew up, while an abundance-mentality person will use their philosophy to create excessive amounts of net worth while not spending a dime. The point is, you and your spouse each have a money language.

The question is, do you understand each other's language? Are you able to pull together in spite of your different vantage points to partner the others' strengths with your weaknesses and vice versa? Let me give you a few relational points that will help you as you learn each other's language.

**Have a Dream Meeting**

In mine and my wife's case, we had never sat down and discussed what we dreamed about for our future. All we knew were societal norms that we assumed we should have. And because we knew we had very limited income, we thought debt was our answer to the things that seemed normal around us. It was the only way some of our desires would ever come to pass in our present situation. We wanted to look successful even though our income couldn't support the things we thought made us look that way. This was our way of looking blessed, though we didn't realize *it wasn't God* blessing us. We were *blessing ourselves* and then begging God to help us make the payments.

When we sat down and started talking about what truly meant something to us, we discovered that the things we thought made us look like we had it all together were actually creating stress and fear in our marriage that was trying to choke us out. We had to determine to believe God at His Word:

> *Proverbs 22:7 ESV*[39]
> *The rich rules over the poor,*
> *and the borrower is the slave of the lender.*

We decided that what actually made us feel peace was the following: eradicating debt and not owing anyone anything, a margin in our monthly budget that resulted in a healthy emergency fund in case of difficulties, and enough set aside to be spontaneously generous should God ask us to give. None of those things were true for us at that moment, which meant we had to do something about it. We had to decide on our values, what mattered to us as a couple, and what we were going to do about it.

You and your spouse need to plan an evening, take the kids to a babysitter, make a nice meal, and sit down to talk about what you dream of doing in the short-term and long-term future of your marriage. What matters to you financially? What things would you like to purchase someday? Where would you like to live? What kind of a house do you want to live in? What kind of car would you like to drive? What kind of projects do you want to give to? What kind of education do you want to be able to provide for your children? Be very specific. It doesn't even need to be reasonable or attainable today. It's just a chance for you to share your values and dreams with one another so you can hear one another's hearts.

Here's a very important key: do not ridicule your spouse's dream or values. It's there for a reason, and it will help you to understand them in a new and very important way. This is the only way you can have unity as you move forward in the area of finances. Remember, you are developing an understanding of your spouse's language around money.

The first thing my wife and I did as we started to understand our individual and differing dreams was attend *Fi-*

nancial Peace University, Dave Ramsey's 9-week course, which began to give us a plan on how to possibly reach some of those goals. The remainder of this chapter will outline the foundation of the Ramsey Solutions plan, and taking this class is my recommendation to take your financial unity to the next level as you grow as a couple in the area of personal finances.

Once you dream together, it's time to start framing a strategy for how to see your dreams become a possibility.

## Budget Committee Meeting

The next thing we did after we started to dream about what we'd like to see come to pass in the area of our finances was to sit down and be extremely honest about where our finances were. We developed a budget committee that was composed of my wife and me. Both of us needed to know the following information in order to start the process of healing and trusting one another again:

1. *What is our actual monthly net income (after tax)?*

Knowing your actual monthly income is important because you have to know how many dollars you have to work with in your monthly budget.

2. *What are ALL of our monthly living expenses (housing, utilities, subscriptions, groceries, fuel, etc.)?*

As odd as it may seem, it can take a married couple several months to figure this out. You can't leave anything out. In my experience, automated payments and subscriptions have a tendency to hide due to a lack of organization. Though the goal is to have these in your budget (which we'll design next), if you do miss an expense, simply put it in, adjust the math, and keep going.

> 3. *Are there any expenses that have been hidden by one spouse or the other that need to be disclosed?*

As we discussed in the last chapter, it's very important to start looking at your finances as one unit. In almost every case, a couple should operate from the combined income and the agreed-upon expenses brought by both spouses. Your income and outgo should flow through a *shared bank account*. You married each other because of love, respect, and mutual trust. It is a contradiction to say that you are *one* if you refuse to combine your finances and operate your household together. If you are willing to share a bed, you should be willing to share your income and expenses. (Some exceptions may exist in the case of a couple being married later in life, with the unique situation where a prenuptial agreement may have been a useful tool due to family dynamics. This, however, is a very rare occurrence and should be considered an extreme *last* resort.)

You need to have a very vulnerable conversation about your combined and individual debts and any other hidden expenses you may have been keeping from one another. Healing can only take place in full disclosure. Otherwise, trust is compromised. If you refuse full disclosure in your finances, your spouse may feel disrespected at best, and cheated at worst. In fact, it's not uncommon for a spouse who has been deceived to undergo the same emotions that are felt when an infidelity occurs. A term for this could be "financial infidelity." It is vital that you *not* commit financial adultery against your spouse. Be honest and vulnerable. Own your mistakes and failures. Apologize to your spouse and watch God bring you together in unity.

Make a *Budget Committee Meeting* a monthly priority before your next paychecks arrive. That way, you have a roadmap in place before your dollars start running away.

## The Zero-Based Budget

The single most important part of your financial unity and success is going to be centered on what is called the Zero-Based Budget. My recommendation is that you write your first couple of months' worth of budgets on an actual piece of paper that you can both see. But eventually, an amazing tool to use is the EveryDollar® app from Ramsey Solutions. The basic access to this app is free, but additional features can be added at a cost. You can share a login so that both of you can see the budget in living detail on your smartphone every day as you update your expenses and income.

Before we talk about how to create the budget, let's set something in place that is very important. Budgets are not just for people struggling with their finances. Budgets are for wise people who want to be good stewards of what they are given. A budget is your instruction for your money's use every month *for the rest of your life*. It's literally your plan on paper every time you get paid. You will always have a budget for the rest of your life. This will be your key to financial success, and this will be your key to marital unity in the area of finances.

One more important note: once you make your budget, you have to actually *do* the budget. I can't tell you how often I've coached an individual or a couple in the area of their finances, and when I meet with them the following month, they didn't follow the plan they made. The goal is not to make a beautiful budget on paper so you can admire it. The goal is to make a beautiful budget on paper that accomplishes what you created it to do. But that only happens when you, as a team, *do* the budget as planned. If things change throughout the month, adjust the budget. Just realize that you don't get a pass on math just because your situation changes. Your budget has to balance. If an expense is higher than you expected, or something comes in you didn't plan for, you must adjust your budget so it still equals $0 at the end of the month.

This brings us to the Zero-Based Budget. A Zero budget does *not* mean you have zero dollars. What it means is that **your income minus your expenses equals zero.** You plan your budget before you get paid, so when you get paid, you simply implement that plan...including savings goals. Let me demonstrate with mock, round numbers as an example:

## Example Income: $4,000 per month

From this income, you will subtract your expenses until you reach zero:

## ZERO BASED BUDGET

| TITHES: | $400.00 | $3600.00 |
| --- | --- | --- |
| RENT: | $1350.00 | $2250.00 |
| GROCERIES: | $400.00 | $1850.00 |
| ELECTRICITY: | $150.00 | $1700.00 |
| WATER: | $25.00 | $1675.00 |
| FUEL: | $225.00 | $1450.00 |
| CREDIT CARD: | $150.00 | $1300.00 |
| CAR PAYMENT: | $500.00 | $800.00 |
| MEDICAL BILL: | $200.00 | $600.00 |
| INSURANCE: | $100.00 | $500.00 |
| SCHOOL FEES: | $75.00 | $425.00 |
| INTERNET: | $100.00 | $325.00 |
| FUN MONEY: | $200.00 | $125.00 |
| SAVINGS: | $125.00 | $0 |

Often, I'll have people protest this strategy because they have a unique pay schedule or they have a variable income. This does not give you an out for doing the budget. It's even *more* important to budget if your income fluctuates. How do you budget a variable income or unusual pay cycle? You base your initial budget on the lowest possible estimate of what your income might be, making sure the least important things are at the bottom and the most important things get paid first. If you get paid more than you thought, you keep adding items on the bottom until you get to your actual income amount. Remember, this is your budget, which means if you need to adjust it, you can. As long as you get to zero at the end, you're doing it right.

## What If We're In Crisis?

Ramsey Solutions encourages a household to base its initial, most important budget items on the Four Walls:

- Food
- Shelter
- Transportation
- Utilities

If you have a shortfall, the most important things need to come first in your budget. Make sure you and your family can eat, that you have a roof over your head, that you can get to work by paying for transportation, and are able to keep the electricity and water on at home. The rest can wait. It is amazing how often people will pay pesky creditors first and leave their family hungry.

As more money comes in, have the rest of your expenses listed in order of importance. Pay each one down on that list until you run out of money. In this way, the least important thing is what falls off the bottom.

## What About Biblical Giving?

God makes it very clear to give to God off the top of your budget as your first priority from your income.

> *Leviticus 27:30 NKJV*[39]
> *30 And all the tithe of the land, whether of the seed of the land or of the fruit of the tree, is the Lord's. It is holy to the Lord.*

> *2 Corinthians 9:7-8 NKJV[40]*
> *7 So let each one give as he purposes in his heart, not grudgingly or of necessity; for God loves a cheerful giver.*
> *8 And God is able to make all grace abound toward you, that you, always having all sufficiency in all things, may have an abundance for every good work.*

The Biblical baseline is to give 10% of your household income to the local storehouse, which is your local church. Offerings are above and beyond the 10% and are given to other institutions or projects. Why does God want you to give to your local church? Because that is where your family of believers are reaching your neighborhoods with the Gospel of Jesus Christ. Your contributed funds help advance the Kingdom of God, keep your leaders fed, take care of the poor, and take care of the place of worship in the community where you reside (Deuteronomy 26:12-13).

This may seem very simplistic, but it should be. If you make sure God is the top line item on your budget, you'll never miss giving to Him. Often, God doesn't get honored in finances because He is the bottom line of the budget. Make sure God is first. In my life, nothing else gets paid until God is put first. It's my act of worship and trust in God. As you notice in my mock budget above, the giving category is the first line item. God asks us to give because He made us in His image and calls us to emulate Him. Remember, God so loved the world that He *gave* His only Son (John 3:16). If we reflect God's character, then obedience to God's instruction to give will be our top priority.

You'll never regret being generous. It establishes a pattern of what kind of character you want to have long into your future. Give a little today and you'll train yourself to give a lot in your future. Be the answer to the needs around you, and watch God bless you abundantly in order to keep blessing others around you. It's a cycle. It's a joy. It's in God's Word.

## Recommendation for The Future

There are obviously many details involved in personal finances that we are not able to cover in detail in one chapter. Each couple has nuances that may require a unique approach, and there are things beyond the budget and communication that will take your dreams and goals to the next level. Let these principles be the foundation you start building on, and follow these steps:

- *Schedule your dream meeting*
- *Have your budget committee meeting every month*
- *Do your Zero-Based Budget every month before you get paid, and then obey it.*

Go through Dave Ramsey's Financial Peace University as soon as possible. This will help you take further steps toward financial peace and financial freedom.

## MARRIAGE ACTIVATION 12

Money is a tool. It can be used to fuel our dreams and help those around us. As you go through these activations together, allow yourself to dream with each other and with Jesus for what your finances will look like going forward.

1. Schedule your Dream Meeting. Right now, pull out your calendars and put it on your schedule. Write down the date and time here: _____
2. Now schedule your Monthly Budget Committee Meeting (remember to do this *before* your paycheck arrives to ensure you have a plan in place): _____
3. When you have your Monthly Budget Committee Meeting, you can use the following budget form as an example to get you started. Feel free to make changes as needed.

# BUDGET

| INCOME | AMOUNT |
|--------|--------|
|        |        |
|        |        |
|        |        |
|        |        |
|        |        |
|        | TOTAL: |

| DEBT | PAID |
|------|------|
|      |      |
|      |      |
|      |      |
|      |      |
|      |      |
|      | TOTAL: |

| FIXED EXPENSES | BUDGET | SPENT |
|----------------|--------|-------|
|                |        |       |
|                |        |       |
|                |        |       |
|                |        |       |
|                |        |       |
|                |        |       |
|                |        |       |
|                |        |       |
|                |        | TOTAL: |

| VARIABLE EXPENSES | BUDGET | SPENT |
|-------------------|--------|-------|
|                   |        |       |
|                   |        |       |
|                   |        |       |
|                   |        |       |
|                   |        |       |
|                   |        |       |
|                   |        |       |
|                   |        |       |
|                   |        |       |
|                   |        |       |
|                   |        |       |
|                   |        |       |
|                   |        | TOTAL: |

| SAVINGS | SAVED |
|---------|-------|
|         |       |
|         |       |
|         |       |
|         |       
|         | TOTAL: |

TOTAL BUDGET [    ] − TOTAL SPENT [    ] = [    ]

# CHAPTER 13

## SETTING THE FOUNDATION FOR A GODLY HOME

In James Dobson's book *Love Must Be Tough*, he tells of a 6th grade teacher who gave her 30 students a writing assignment. Each student was asked to finish the sentence: "I wish…" The teacher was expecting answers like "I wish I had a new bike, gaming system, a dog…"

She was shocked that 20 out of 30 students in the class made their response in reference to their dysfunctional families.

- "I wish my parents wouldn't fight."
- "I wish my father would come home."
- "I wish my mom didn't have a boyfriend."
- "I wish I got straight A's so my dad would love me."
- "I wish I had one mom and dad so the other kids wouldn't make fun of me."
- "I wish I had an M-1 rifle so I could shoot the people who make fun of me.

She was shocked at the level of conflict these children lived in.

*James 4:1 NASB[41]*
*What is the source of quarrels and conflicts among you...?*

I would like to propose that if a family is going to be what God wants it to be, both parents need to agree on a philosophy of child-rearing and stand together no matter what. This is easily said, but difficult to put into practice. You both come from different upbringings, even if your childhood family life was good. Different does not mean bad. It just means *different*. But as you embark on this journey of marriage, you will still have to deal with different perspectives and ideas of how you should do things. Just because something worked in your family growing up doesn't mean it will work in this new family you are creating with your spouse. You have to decide how *you* are going to do things in *your* family.

We are living in a day that is increasingly difficult for families. The traditional family is breaking down as the flow of society is working against it.

Alvin Toffler, author of *The Third Wave,* estimated that only 7% of Americans live in what used to be considered normal: a husband, a wife, and 2 or more children.

Christian values are under relentless attack in today's culture. What is on the TV when the kids get home from school? What messages are kids getting from their peers and teachers at school and in other social avenues? They are very often being told that drugs, sex, and alcohol are the way to happiness, and homosexuality is a completely acceptable alternative lifestyle. Most alarming, they are being told that the Bible and its stories are unreliable fables that are neither logical or real.

It is going to take more to protect our children than just taking them to Sunday School once a week. The discipleship and raising of your children is your responsibility. You cannot leave it to the children's pastor at your church, just as you cannot expect your children to eat only once a week.

Let's be creative in instilling Godly values in our kids. Studying the Bible doesn't have to be completely boring for your children. What were some ways you enjoyed learning about the Word of God when you were a child? Or if you did not grow up in the church, how would you have liked to learn about God when you were your children's age? Make it fun *and* educational. Pray together as a family. Read the Bible together. Find a devotional that is age-appropriate and start instilling those values into your children.

The *Listen* app, produced by the Assemblies of God, offers age-aligned material for the whole family. You can enjoy learning the same material presented at different reading levels to accommodate understanding and foster discussion. This is just one resource that can help you as you forge your way to becoming a God-centered family.

Before you know it, your children will be grown, and it will be time to release them into the world. What kinds of tools do you want them to have when they face this world? They must be prepared so they won't be swept away by the ever-shifting tides of culture. What kind of morals and character do you want them to possess before they leave your care and start their own lives as adults?

Relationship with Jesus is the first step in creating a God-focused and God-driven home.

**Rules Provide Security**

The reality of boundaries and rules concerning children is this: they truly are like little velociraptors. If you have ever watched the movie *Jurassic Park*, the scene where the professional hunter takes all of the visitors out to the velociraptor pen illustrates this point perfectly. The visitors get to see a cow being lowered into the pen for the feeding process. During this process, the hunter turns to all of the visitors and says, "That's why we have to put them in a pen of this magnitude...They were testing the fences for weaknesses systematically. They remember..."

That is exactly how children are the minute they come into this world. They are always checking the barriers, parameters, and restrictions that parents put on them in order to try to find a weakness. We all know this is true if we were to be honest with ourselves, because we were once children, too. We did the same to our parents.

Although this process is universal to everyone and every culture, it still catches new parents off guard. We all need rules, boundaries, and expectations in order to be healthy, successful contributors to society, and this starts in the home with our children. Our Heavenly Father knew this about us as well. That's why He created an entire book, called the Bible, to protect us with those same guidelines, boundaries, and directions. Every parent knows a child needs to be protected. The problem comes in with the day-in and day-out grind of these ever-testing little velociraptors trying to find a weakness in our parenting style. Our desire is to show them love and protection so that they do not bring harm to themselves or others unknowingly. That is always the true motive of rules. They are set in place to offer protection. It's exhausting for any parent to stay consistent in establishing boundaries, but honestly, that is our job.

Over many years of counseling, there have been a few consistent themes that have come up concerning this issue. First, parents just get weary over time. Next, parents are very insecure and lonely. Instead of raising children with the hope that they will be great contributing individuals to society, they have children to fill the void of their own loneliness, so they can have a friend. This is always problematic.

God did not give children to parents to fill a void of insecurity and loneliness within them. God gave children to parents so that they would raise them in His ways and desires. The biggest areas of conflict that arise in the home seem to be those two issues: weariness and loneliness. Take a really close look at your current relationship with your children. If you are using them to fill some emotional void in your life, such as loneliness and rejection, you will ultimately damage your children. They do not have the emotional capacity to fulfill your needs. So, let me make this big, bold statement: you have not been given children to be their best friends. You have been given children because God believed you could be parents to them. With that comes boundaries, rules, and restrictions. Don't forget that. Friendship can come later.

The following are practical suggestions that will make it easier (for you and for your children) to have a healthy vantage point in life:

1. **Make the Marriage the Center of the Home, Not the Kids.**

This is the classic mistake of allowing priorities to get totally out of order. As we've touched on before, God must come first in your life if you want to have closeness, intimacy, health, and strength in any of your relationships, especially in the marriage relationship. The second person on your priority list is your spouse. Third is your children. If at any point your children come before your spouse, you have gotten things out of order, and dysfunction always follows.

---

> The above statement may seem counterintuitive, especially as a mom. Your whole life seems to get wrapped up in keeping these tiny humans alive and making sure they grow up to be viable and responsible members of society. But what happens when your first priority becomes your children? Your husband inevitably feels pushed to the wayside. What began as an exciting adventure can quickly turn into resentment.
> 
> Let us get something straight right now. Your husband is your first priority (after God), not your

children. If you allow the marriage relationship to stagnate and break down, your husband is not the only one who will suffer in the process. Research shows that when a husband and wife are strong and they display a loving relationship and united front, the children reap the benefits. When a child sees their father loving and serving their mother and cherishing her first, it boosts their sense of security, emotional well-being, and their understanding of what a healthy relationship is supposed to look like.

I tried very hard to make sure that my priorities stayed in the right order after my husband and I had our first child. I didn't do it perfectly. Honestly, I'm not really sure how anyone survives the sleepless nights and postpartum depression, or the many changes that overtake your life. Literally, it's by the grace of God and leaning so heavily on my husband and the rest of our family that I made it through. My husband was amazing. Even with all the crazy he had to put up with as we navigated my hormones and our sleep deprivation, he stayed constant.

It would have been so easy to slip into forgetting his needs and solely focus on the baby's. He was so patient with me, but I'm not going to say it wasn't difficult. I would not have wanted to do it without him.

The truth is, those hard seasons don't last forever. Believe me, I thought it would never end. But there was so much joy that came from that season as well, and even though I heard it about a million times, this season really does go so fast. The days go slowly, but the years go fast.

When you come out on the other side and your kids become more independent, how is your marriage going to fare? Will it be stronger or weaker? Will there be a wall of resentment built between you, or will you have built a tower of strength, where you stand back-to-back and take life's challenges together, providing a safe place for yourselves and your children?

— NICOLE BOYD

---

## 2. Kids Need a Daily Dose of God's Word

*Psalm 119:11 NIV[42]*
*Your word I have hidden in my heart,*
*That I might not sin against You.*

There is no way in this world that anyone, regardless of age, can function or live without having a daily deposit of God's Word. That is why it is so important that at a very early age, children begin to understand the discipline and importance of God's Word. It will help them to navigate this world for the rest of their lives. It's a beautiful thing for a child to see their mother participating in her own private altar. It's also a powerful and wonderful thing for a child to get up and walk in the living room and see their father sitting in his chair with his Bible in his lap. However, if all your children ever see is the privacy of their parents' personal Bible study and growth, there will come a day when they will depart from it simply because they were never *included*. They were never taught how to do it for themselves. That is why it is so important to have a family altar, or family devotion time, where the Word of God becomes the light and guiding force for the family through every facet of life together. This is what they will lean on after they have left the home. It may not be immediate, but that is why God's Word says this: *"Train up a child in the way they should go, and they will not soon depart from it." (Proverbs 22:6)* This is such a vital scripture, because there is so much truth within it. It is the training from the Word of God that puts the spiritual compass within a child.

---

> It is never too early to start filling them with the Word of God. It doesn't matter if they don't understand everything. *I* don't even understand everything, and I don't think we will for the rest of eternity. That is the beauty of our God—there will always be new facets of His character and overwhelming beauty that we get to learn about!
>
> It is your job to instill the values and love of the Lord in your children. They are a gift from God. It is so easy to forget that they are your mission field before any other ministry opportunity. As a mom, it can be hard to feel like you are making any real difference in the world. Don't overlook the fact that your husband and children are your first ministry. Much of

what your kids learn in the early years comes down to what you choose to instill in them.

— NICOLE BOYD

## 3. Let Freedom Reign: Transitioning From Childhood to Adulthood

This is yet again a very difficult season of being a parent. You've poured your heart and soul into raising your kids, but so often, people—especially moms—have a hard time letting go. As they transition into adulthood, it can be hard to know how to make the switch from being a parent to a friend, but that is what you want. So many times, parents get this backward. You want your children to like you, to have a friendship with you. When kids are young, this is detrimental. When they are growing and learning, they need a parent—not a best friend. They can find their best friends at school or church. They need your guidance and discipline to grow into the people they were meant to be.

However, when they get older and start to near the place where they are entering adulthood, you can start making that transition to friendship. You are able to start giving them more trust, as they earn it, and your support helps give them the confidence they need to go out into the world on their own.

During this time, you will need your spouse

more than ever. Cling to your spouse. I've often heard that empty-nest syndrome is no joke...

— NICOLE BOYD

---

If any of you have ever watched the movie *Braveheart*, in the very last climactic scene, as William Wallace is being martyred for his revolt against England, he yells out one powerful word. He screams, *"Freedom!"* There will come a point when all of the protection, all of the training, and all of the guidance that you have given will need to be tested in the real world. If you don't allow them their freedom, your children will feel like you don't trust them, and that you're a hypocrite. You want your freedom, but you will not allow them theirs.

This is a very dangerous time for both the children and the parents, because that transition is something that we can never fully prepare for. This transition doesn't necessarily have an age or date assigned to it. But as all of us should remember, there was a time in our lives when we began to push back at rules and guidelines that no longer matched or added up concerning our protection. This is a very critical time within a family's process. This is the time when all parents have to come to the realization that their seven-year-old little baby girl isn't seven anymore. She's *seventeen*. I understand that for many, this is an easier transition than for others. That's why it's imperative that you be very watchful of both the maturity level and trust level your child has earned from you, and allow them an opportunity to live life and make their own mistakes.

The counseling that I have done surrounding this has been very eye-opening. It's at this time that a lot of marriages start to be tested beyond what they've ever been before. Especially if you have one parent who is acting in a healthy role, while having the other parent utilize their relationship with their children as a crutch. If there is a parent with an unhealthy view, that they are using their children as some kind of healing in their hearts to hold off dealing with insecurities and rejections, there are going to be problems.

The parent who has been using their child for their emotional support will find themselves absolutely unable to set their children free. It is not because their children aren't prepared, but because the parent cannot handle the thought of them having freedom. They fear the thought that they will be left without the comfort they need to offset the battle they have ahead in dealing with their struggles with rejection, insecurity, and pain. This is where the negative role becomes evident, where this child (or children) have been fulfilling the needs of this very insecure parent. This is going to cause a disturbance in the force, unlike anything their marriage has seen before. This parent, who has been burying their rejection and loneliness issues, will suddenly have a huge magnifying glass on the real problems that have been hiding under the surface.

The marriage, at this time, is in a make-it-or-break-it state, because this individual has been using their children as an emotional support system for their insecurities, and there is no way of hiding that anymore. The parent who has been unknowingly abusing their parental relationship with their child is going to have to deal with their issues. It is a difficult road, but it must be done if they are going to continue to have a relationship with their children. It must also be done if they are going to have a healthy relationship with their spouse.

That is why so many of our young adults have not been leaving home. The parent who has been using their child as an emotional security blanket purposefully does not prepare them to go out into the world so they can continue in their unfair role. The statistics are overwhelming in our culture at how many adult children live at home because they are absolutely overwhelmed with fear of going out into the world. It is unfortunate, because this emotionally abusive parent has controlled them all of their life. This is not protection of the child. It is selfishness birthed from insecurity and the spirit of rejection. (This subject is discussed in depth in another book I've written. I highly recommend this parent getting the book, *Break Free.*)\*

### 4. Pray for them every day.

> At the end of the day, your children are going to grow up, and they are going to leave and start families of their own. Prayer must be the foundation you build on, from the time they take their first breath and for the rest of their lives.
>
> Pray for your children. Pray for their future and that they would give their lives to God early and serve Him all the days of their lives. Pray for their

---

\* Break Free Book: https://a.co/d/hhJDf68

> future spouses and that God would protect and prepare that person for them, even when your kids are young. We cannot comprehend how important and what a difference a life of prayer makes.
>
> — NICOLE BOYD

All of us must understand that prayer is not an automatically learned response to the challenges we face in this world. The enemy has caused our communication with the Lord to feel very awkward. That is why the parents' role in training their children to pray is so vital. It can start as simply as having your child pray over a meal, even if they have to repeat a prayer in the beginning. You speak it for them, and have them repeat until they get the idea.

When sin entered the world in Genesis, one of the main areas that was affected within humanity was our natural ability to be able to communicate with our Father God. Parents need to be very proactive and patient in displaying how wonderful and easy prayer can be. I don't want to push too heavily on one gender, but I'm going to do it here. Men struggle with this most of the time. They tend to have a very inhibited approach to their relationship with God, which is very unfortunate for them and for their children.

This must change. Fathers, it is through you that children decide, many times, what to fear and what not to fear. It is you they are watching when unsettling situations and circumstances happen in the family and in life. If they see that you are hesitant, nonchalant, and even flippant about wanting to pray at any given time, trust me, they will follow that same example. It is time for the fathers and men to step up to their role as the prayer warriors over their homes, their children, and their families. Stop making excuses for why you don't do it. Stop making empty promises about when you plan to start. Just start praying now.

I experienced the power of how a personal and purposeful sensitivity to the Holy Spirit saved my son's life in his teenage years.

I was in a private time of prayer on a Saturday night before part of our family was to leave on our annual elk hunting vacation. My son had gotten a summer job and needed to work throughout the week, which caused him to have to leave at a later date instead of with the rest of the family after church on Sunday. Usually, we all went together for a week to prepare and camp before the opening day of elk season. My son was scheduled to leave Thursday afternoon by himself to drive up and meet us at camp. I felt unsettled while I was praying about the services the next day, but didn't quite know what it was about.

In the middle of the night, I had a vivid prophetic dream: I was actually hovering over the top of my son's little white Ford Ranger as he was traveling between Prineville and John Day through the Fossil Canyon on his way to elk camp. I was able to see inside the cab of his truck as he was rocking out and singing at the top of his lungs to the music blaring from the radio. I was flying above my son's pickup around the curves and corners of this very steep canyon with a dry river bed off to the right. My son came up on a very slow-moving vehicle, which caused him to become very impatient and frustrated. I was trying to tell him, even in my dream, to calm down. My thoughts were that he's not going to a fire, he's already on vacation, and to *just relax*. But the longer this vehicle progressed up the incline, the slower it got, which obviously brought intense frustration and irritation to my son. Finally, he lost all control of his patience and decided to pass on a blind curve. Because of my perspective flying above his vehicle, I could see further down the road and instantly realized that he was going to have a head-on collision with a large box truck if he did this maneuver. As much as I screamed in my dream for him to stay in his lane, he made the maneuver anyway.

And exactly what I had feared happened. As he tried to swerve to miss the box truck, it squarely caught him on the front side of his vehicle, causing it to roll down the canyon. As I floated over the top of all this terrifying action, on the fourth roll-over, he was ejected from his vehicle and flew hundreds of feet to his death in the bedrock of the dry creek bed below. I was able to position myself over the top of him, only to see massive amounts of blood coming from his head and his lifeless body.

This obviously was such a traumatic dream that I instantly woke up. I sat there for quite some time, praying desperately for what the dream meant and what I needed to do to protect my son. Later that morning, as I got up to prepare to go to the church and preach for our two services, I reached over and shook my wife awake. All I told her was I had had a dream (I did not give her the details or the context of the dream, other than to say that our son was in a massive car accident coming to the elk woods this

Thursday), and she would be staying behind that day to travel with him later in the week.

She was obviously disappointed with this decision, as I was taking two or three of her days of vacation to babysit her almost-grown son. But after looking at the seriousness and intensity of my gaze, she finally smiled and said, "I understand, no problem."

Throughout the week, I was haunted by the dream on numerous occasions, and immediately went to intercessory prayer concerning it. I was very anxious about Thursday's arrival and what could happen now that, not only was my son coming up in his Ford Ranger, but his mother would be a passenger. I called early Thursday morning just to let my wife know a few small details of the dream. I told her not to tell my son about it, and she agreed. We scheduled a time to meet in the city of John Day in order to have an early dinner and to pick up some supplies to take back to camp. This was back when cell phone service was very spotty and difficult in the mountains. Finally, I was able to reach them just as they were coming through a little town called Dayville, which was only about twenty to thirty minutes away from me. My wife was very short and distraught on the phone call and only said, "Your son is messed up and will need to talk to you immediately when we get to the restaurant."

I said, "Okay, I will be prepared." When they arrived, it was very evident that both of them had been crying, and something very emotionally disturbing had happened. My son walked right up to me as tears continued to stream down his cheeks, and he said, "Please, Dad, get in your truck. I need to talk to you right now." I sent his mother and my daughter into the restaurant to order for us, and we took a drive to fill a propane tank. The minute we got in the truck, he said, "Dad, I need to have every detail of your dream, please."

So I proceeded to tell him exactly what I had seen in my dream, which only escalated his emotions. He took two or three great big breaths and said, "Let me tell you what happened. We were in the canyon between Mitchel, Oregon, and the turn-off to Spray. I got behind a large motorcycle with a male and female rider. She was taking pictures of the canyon walls and the scenic vistas while they were driving, and she was continually asking her husband to slow down. They were going *horrifically* slow."

He went on, "I finally reached a point where my patience had run out. Even though I knew I wasn't in a safe area to pass, I couldn't handle it any longer, so I started to go around them. The minute I did, Mom started screaming at the top of her lungs to get over and not do it. We both know she never does this. But she just kept on until I finally stomped on the brakes and moved back over. At that very moment, from around the corner came a box truck. I know without a doubt, I would have hit it head-on. Dad, thank you for being sensitive enough in your prayer time for God to give you this dream, cause I'm very sure I would not be here on this planet right now if you had not told Mom to stay home and ride with me."

At that moment, we both sat in silence. It was finally broken when I reached over and wrapped him in a hug and said this, "God never fails, never gives up, and never lets go."

By the way, we had pizza for lunch, and all rejoiced that

we were together. This is why I'm so adamant about intercessory prayer, and specifically, fathers, knowing how to pray. Everything must flow from your personal prayer life. If your relationship with Jesus is strong, it will overflow into your marriage, which will in turn overflow into your family.

## MARRIAGE ACTIVATION 13

Prayer is a foundation for your marriage and family that cannot be overlooked. We may not always see the fruit of our prayers, but rest assured, those prayers do not come back without accomplishing powerful things in the spirit and in the natural.

1. Do you pray for your children as a couple? If not, set a time you can pray for your children every day, whether separately or together. Then set a time to pray for them together as their parents every week.
2. What are the dreams you have for your children? Take some time to write those things down now. This does not necessarily mean what kind of job you hope they have or what you'd like to see them accomplish in sports or school. What are the deep things, *the eternal things*, that you would pray over your children?

3. Take some time to listen to the Holy Spirit and ask Him what He is speaking over your children. (I, Nicole, keep a journal for each of our children and have added prophetic words and prayers to those journals since before either of them were born. I've asked family members to write down prophetic words for them at different times. When they graduate high school, I will give them their journal as a gift. Starting that legacy of speaking those encouraging and prophetic words over their lives is invaluable. You don't have to follow my example, but I would encourage you to start writing down some verses and prayers that you could pray over your children.)
4. Lastly, I want you to get some anointing oil and pray over every member of your family and your house. If there has been anything, such as strife, contentions, frustration, anger, or disunity, take authority over them in the name of Jesus. Go around your home and anoint the doorposts of every room. Pick a time at some point in the next month, perhaps at the dinner table, to read 1 Corinthians 11:23-26. Then, take communion together as a whole family.

***Joshua 24:15 NIV*[43]**

**15** *"But if serving the Lord seems undesirable to you, then choose for yourselves this day whom you will serve, whether the gods your ancestors served beyond the Euphrates, or the gods of the Amorites, in whose land you are living. But as for me and my household, we will serve the Lord."*

# CHAPTER 14

## WHEN YOU'RE CALLED TO PARENT SOMEONE ELSE'S CHILD

**BY BILLY AND KRISTEN**

### Plan-C: Our Perspective

There are lots of plans you will come across in a marriage and in life in general. This is how we have looked at our blended family, from the other side of some of our toughest struggles. We think there are often three plans for marriage, and they are as follows:

- Plan A: Get married once—stay married.
- Plan B: Get divorced—don't get remarried.
- Plan C: Divorce and remarry—be aware that this is Plan C and has some unique challenges.

Keep in mind that however hard you think Plan C is going to be, *it will be even harder*. This is not God's initial and ideal plan for marriage. A breakup and the process of healing and starting over bring substantial challenges that require a lot of prayer, a lot of patience, and an abundance of understanding. This arrangement should only be entered into with lots of quality Christian counseling, a *thus-saith-the-Lord*, and a lifelong commitment to each other: forever, for always, no matter what.

Each situation will vary with the involvement of participants and children in your family. This is our perspective based on our own situation. These are the top five challenges that we experienced:

1. **Negative Involvement From Outside Influences.**

This could be family or the other parents, aunts, uncles, grandparents, and even your friends. Basically, anybody who interacts with your children, or those they may be exposed to, will feel like they have a right to bring input, even when they have no clue about your individual and specific situation.

Not all of your friends and family may be on board with this new marriage. The negative influence that outside individuals may have on your children will have an effect on the daily life and functioning of your home. This is especially true if you have been awarded the majority of the custody of the children. In particular, the other parents can have a negative effect on your children in helping them adjust to a blended family life. If the outside parent does not agree with your choice of marital partner, they may talk in a derogatory manner about you or the new step-parent. There will most certainly be tension, animosity, and criticism of your decision to remarry. They may even expect the children to show a false sense of loyalty toward them by not honoring or respecting the authority of the new step-parent in the home. This just makes it harder on your children when they have to go back and forth, spending time with each household. It is important to try to get the ex-spouse to understand that maturity and wisdom should come before their feelings and emotions when talking to the children about this new adventure. It is vital to do what is best for the children.

2. **Standing United as a Blended Family.**

Before blending your family together, it is our recommendation to sit down together and come up with a way that you are going to try and lead and guide your children as a new family unit. We had many family meetings on the living room floor with all the children when something came up that involved possible dysfunction in the family, or decisions needed to be made that would affect all of us. That way, the children knew this decision was coming from both of us and that we were a united front. We had already agreed together on what was going to be said, so that there would be no going to one parent or the other to try to get them to change their minds or give a different answer. This pitting one parent against the other is very common in blended families because of the delicate nature of the new situation and multiple people having input into every decision. People need to remember we're dealing with kids here, at the end of the day. Everybody wants what they want, even if they must manipulate to get it. What really has to be considered is what's best for the child, not the other people. No matter what happens, you must stand your ground in firmness and in love. Never allow your children and step-children to pit you against one another. It's vital that you remain united in all things.

### 3. Solidifying Your Parameters and Boundaries

Make sure that you and your new spouse have clear parameters and boundaries for the rules of the house and that you both agree on them ahead of time. These rules and boundaries must be presented to the children together, again in a united front. The purpose of this may seem obvious, but you are bringing two sets of ideals, two sets of standards, and two sets of rules into one place. Because of that, you have to navigate coming up with a brand new set of parameters and boundaries together as one blended family. This will be the make-or-break of the success of any blended family. Trust us, we know. It is not that rules, boundaries, and parameters won't be tested in a Plan A family, because they will. They are accentuated many times over in a blended family due to the fact that there's a restart that was never meant to happen. All restarts come with a plethora of nuances and struggles no one ever anticipated because every family's DNA is specific to itself, and that's what you're creating. You're trying to establish a new DNA from one that had already been established.

## 4. Discipline and Correction Must Have a Plan

When the discipline comes from the non-biological parent, it is hard for the children to receive it well (especially if they have involvement from influences that are not acting in maturity or in a Christlike manner from outside the new marriage). Discipline is seldom taken well from any child, but when it comes from the non-biological parent (step-parent), it is important that both parents agree and support one another. The children must know the parents are in unity with the discipline chosen, and it must be the exact same expectation from each parent and each disciplining moment.

You must also take into account that your discipline technique cannot differ between the children in the home, whether they are yours or your spouse's. (i.e, The children from *her* side of the family get different treatment than the children on *his* side of the family.) This not only creates resentment between the children themselves, but between the step-children and their new step-parent as well. The rules must be fair for everyone involved, and they must be consistent. Otherwise, you are inviting chaos into your home. Prayerfully consider how best to move forward with discipline. I would advise sitting down with a counselor as a couple and try to think of every detail and scenario that may come up so you can have an unbiased third-party opinion. This way, your home can be filled with peace, understanding, and loving discipline.

### 5. Every Child in the Home Gets Loved the Same

No matter how you initially feel about your new spouse's children, the most important thing that will cause a blended family to be able to function and recreate its own DNA is how you facilitate love. It is so important that all members of the new family feel the same unconditional love toward one another from both marriage partners. They must know that regardless of whether they accept that parent as a parental figure, it doesn't matter. That parent must love them like their very own child, regardless of the child's behavior or acceptance of it. I know this sounds counterintuitive and may even cause conflict for other blended families, but the reason for this is *consistency, consistency, consistency*. Someday, when these children (both the biological and non-biological) grow up, the one thing that they will cherish more than anything is the love that they received from both parents that never wavered.

The children in any kind of family are always comparing themselves to each other. This is compounded when it is a blended family. If you are choosing Plan C, as parents, be especially mindful that the children are going to notice equality (or the lack thereof). When they are young, it's important to enforce the same rules for everybody, striving for the same number of lunch dates with Mom and Dad, and making sure there is equity in the gifts they receive on a holiday. They may use these things as a measuring tool to see if they are loved more or less by their parents. They will be hyper aware of who is getting what, who is doing what with whom, and can use it as a gauge to see if one of the parents is playing favorites.

Coming into a blended family situation can be highly stressful and sometimes fearful for everyone involved, but it is especially true for the children. They need to know that they are loved just as much as they always have been, reassured that the breakdown of the first marriage was not their fault, and that nothing that happened there had anything to do with them. And most importantly, you and your new spouse will love them consistently no matter what.

# MARRIAGE ACTIVATION 14

Being a parent in a blended family comes with its own unique challenges. Take some time to reflect on what is working and what might need some adjustment in how you and your spouse are running your household.

1. What stood out to you that you are doing correctly already, especially if you're a blended family?
2. What stood out to you that you've been doing incorrectly that you may need to adjust immediately?

*Discussion about these two questions cannot be avoided. If you have a blended family, this is what is causing your problems from the outset. You not talking about them and just hoping they will work themselves out on their own will not work.*

3. When was the last time you sat down with your children, as a blended family, and honestly and vulnerably asked them how they felt the family was operating? It might be good to do this as soon as possible if it hasn't happened in a while.

# PART 4
## INTIMACY

*"We don't want our sex life to degenerate into merely a physical act without intimacy and love. No matter how much sex we have, if we don't develop true love and intimacy before sex, then it won't be there after sex."*
—*Wil and Grace Nichols*

# CHAPTER 15

## I OWN YOU

*Song of Songs 6:3 NIV*[44]
*"I am my beloved's and He is mine…"*

When you get married, you lose some of your independence and autonomy. In reality, you lose all of your independence and autonomy. From now on, you are not your own—you belong to your spouse. From now on, you choose one another, and each couple has their own uniqueness in their marriage, which includes how they interact and communicate. But each couple, over time, makes up their own DNA and what works for them.

But when did *belonging* become a bad word? When did it become taboo to say, "They belong to me" or "I belong to you"? Remember, you agreed to marry your spouse, and you thought you meant it, until you heard them say, "You are mine."

What did your promise really mean when you said it at the altar? And when did it become, "No, I don't," or "No, I won't?" This chapter is part of where the title of this book comes from, *I Still Do*. After all the struggles and challenges you have faced, can you still mean it when you say, "I *still* do?"

From a biblical perspective, what did saying "I do" really mean? In a world overrun with discontent and a rebellious spirit, most people didn't mean it when they promised to love, honor, obey, and cherish their spouse. For many people, what they say does not match what they think. This mindset is all too prevalent. What people really mean is, "I belong to no one. No one is going to *own* me or tell me what to do. I am choosing *for this moment* to be married, but if you don't do what I want or you expect too much of me, I will *undo*."

There is a difficulty with this ideology. Subconsciously, you have already created a way to justify your exodus from this relationship and marriage without even realizing it. You have created a thought process that still surrounds you. If your marriage revolves around only you, it will soon not be a marriage. There has to come a point where you realize that there were things done in original marriages by God, and later even by customs throughout the centuries, that were not so barbaric and old-fashioned after all. For instance, the process of the dowry.

The dowry can actually be summed up as a bargaining between two fathers over the marriage and covenant of their children. This included the exchange of goods and services as payment for the bride. Cultures have gotten frustrated with customs like this for a long time because it rendered one of the parties as mere property. But that was not the point in the dowry (at least not in Jewish customs). The point was that the marriage would be not only a covenant but a binding contract. Because the purchase price is being given in full, there would be no refunds. This meant a divorce wasn't even an option. This was also a protection for the wife! I realize many people view all of what was just said as irrelevant when it comes to them and their spouse. After all, we live in the twenty-first century. You may be thinking, "No one bought me. I chose to go into this covenant willingly." All of that is true. What would happen if you allowed yourself for just a moment to realize what God meant when He said, *"The two shall become one"*? The pure and simple definition of God's statement has always been understood as two people surrendering themselves to each other so they now become one. When you boil it down, this means that your spouse owns you and vice versa. This is what makes a marriage whole.

When you got married, it meant you agreed to lay down your life for the other. That may not be how our current culture likes to view marriage, but that is what the Word of God says. *You are not your own.*

> *1 Corinthians 6:17; 19-20 NIV*[45]
> *17 But whoever is united with the Lord is one with him in spirit... 19 Do you not know that your bodies are temples of the Holy Spirit, who is in you, whom you have received from God? You are not your own; 20 you were bought at a price. Therefore honor God with your bodies.*

If you go back and read the broader context of this section of scripture in 1 Corinthians, it is talking about sexual purity (or the lack thereof) and how our bodies are not meant to be joined in sinful relationships. When we have been joined with Christ, can we then be joined with the world and its sinful pleasures? In the same way, you have been joined with your spouse—one flesh—and you are no longer your own. You belong to your spouse, and they belong to you.

Instead of being viewed as a negative word, I see this as wholly comforting. You *belong*. To belong is to be in your proper situation, to be attached to someone by allegiance or birth, and to be in an intimate relationship with the other person.

The marriage union set forth by God is where two people come together willingly and now belong to each other. And, as we've discussed before, this is a picture of what our relationship with God is supposed to look like. We belong to Him, but He also belongs to us. Isn't that mind-blowing? The God of the Universe has limited Himself so He can belong to us just as we belong to Him. We know that Jesus is *our* inheritance. But did you know that we are *His* inheritance as well?

Marriage is a gift from God. It was not good for man to be alone (Genesis 2:18), so God gave us the means to enjoy companionship, intimacy, and the support that comes from a healthy marriage. But it takes laying down your selfishness. It takes laying down what you want, what you dreamed of, your entitlement, and giving yourself wholly to another person. That's really what you were saying when you made your vows. That kind of love can only be modeled with Jesus Christ, the One who gave everything up for you. He bled every last drop of His blood for you in order to redeem you from this world of sin and death. Now you can have an abundant life in Him.

Entitlement is a killer, especially for a marriage. It says, "I deserve," instead of "I serve..."

Do you know why good marriages are on the decline? It's not because divorce is getting so much more common. It's because people aren't getting married in the first place. People are living together because they don't want to be *owned* or live under submission to their spouse or to God.

In more recent history, conventional wisdom has taught that if marriage is relevant at all, living together can certainly let two people know whether they are compatible enough to take the next step into marriage. After all, not getting married is better than getting married and then divorcing, right? Wrong. Unfortunately, this is a concept that people are buying into at alarming rates. Since 1970, the number of cohabitating couples has increased tenfold.

Here are some staggering statistics of cohabitation vs. marriage:

- 1970: 523,000 unmarried couples cohabitating
- 1980: 1.6 million unmarried couples cohabitating
- 2020: 8 million unmarried couples cohabitating[46]

Unfortunately, 63% of young people under 30 believe that cohabitating before marriage increases their chances of having a better marriage later in life.[47] People believe that it is better to get to know each other and see if they're compatible before they take the plunge. They want to pretend to seal the deal before they make the covenant. However, evidence is rapidly mounting that shows this is just not working.

- A woman who is living with a man is more than twice as likely to fall victim to domestic violence.
- Women who are cohabitating suffer from depression at rates three times greater than those of married women.
- Couples who live together and then marry report less satisfaction in their marriage than couples who do not.
- Cohabitating couples who then get married have significantly higher rates of divorce than those who did not live together before marriage.[48]

Unfortunately, the above was the good news.

- 76% say the American Family is in trouble today.
- 84% believe that it is right for a couple who cannot get along to get a divorce.
- Single-parent families are forming at 20 times the rate of dual-parent families.
- 45% of U.S. children will see their parents divorced in the next 5 years.[48]

What happened to the gift of marriage?

God gives you Christ as the foundation of your marriage. *"Welcome one another, therefore, as Christ has welcomed you, for the glory of God" (Romans 15:7).* In a word, live together in the forgiveness of your faults, for without forgiveness no human fellowship, least of all a marriage, can survive. Don't insist on your rights and don't blame each other. Don't judge or condemn each other. Don't find fault with each other. Accept each other as you are and forgive each other every day from the bottom of your hearts. This is what illustrates the gift of marriage. Through all of those specific moments listed above, we see one resonating theme: being married is about serving the other person first. That's why living together is so problematic. It becomes an arrangement based on emotion, sex, and business. It is not based on solemn vows, covenant promises, and forever commitments. That's why this next scripture is so important to understanding the gift of marriage, and what true love really means:

> *1 Corinthians 13:3-8 NKJV*[49]
> *3 And though I bestow all my goods to feed the poor, but have not love, it profits me nothing. 4 Love suffers long and is kind; love does not envy; love does not parade itself, is not puffed up; 5 does not behave rudely, does not seek its own, is not provoked, thinks no evil; 6 does not rejoice in iniquity, but rejoices in the truth; 7 bears all things, believes all things, hopes all things, endures all things. 8 Love never fails.*

To be loved is to belong. Being owned by someone—

belonging to someone—does not need to mean something derogatory or disrespectful. Rather, it is a gift that is a part of God's plan. Letting go of your need for control is when you finally experience true freedom: in your life, in your relationships, but especially in your marriage.

# MARRIAGE ACTIVATION 15

To truly belong is what each of us long for from the time we are children. God has made a way for us to not only belong in the family of God, but in our own family units as we walk out this life of faith with one another. If there has been a wrong mindset in regard to this concept of belonging or being owned by your spouse, allow the Lord to shift your thinking in this area to bring health in your marriage relationship.

## Communion:

*Repeat the following vows aloud in a private setting to one another. Face each other and hold hands:*

> **MEN:** (say aloud) "Today I give myself to you again in marriage. I promise to encourage and inspire you, to laugh with you, and comfort you in times of sorrow and struggle. I promise to love you in good

times and in the bad times. When life seems easy and when it seems hard, when our love is simple, and when it is an effort, and when we have conflicts we've yet to resolve. I promise to cherish you and always hold you with all my love. These things I give you once again on this day, and all the days of our life together."

**WOMEN:** (say aloud) "Today I give myself to you again in marriage. I promise to encourage and inspire you, to laugh with you, and comfort you in times of sorrow and struggle. I promise to love you in good times and in bad. When life seems easy and when it seems hard, when our love is simple, and when it is an effort. Processing through difficult times and seasons, I promise to cherish you, and to always hold you in highest regard. These things I give to you today, and all the days of our life together."

Now, take communion together as specified in Luke:

*Luke 22:14-20 ESV[50]*
*14 And when the hour came, he reclined at table, and the apostles with him. 15 And he said to them, "I have earnestly desired to eat this Passover with you before I suffer. 16 For I tell you I will not eat it until it is fulfilled in the kingdom of God." 17 And he took a cup, and when he had given thanks he said, "Take this, and divide it among yourselves. 18 For I tell you that from now on I will not drink of the fruit of the vine until the kingdom*

*of God comes." **19** And he took bread, and when he had given thanks, he broke it and gave it to them, saying, "This is my body, which is given for you. Do this in remembrance of me." **20** And likewise the cup after they had eaten, saying, "This cup that is poured out for you is the new covenant in my blood.*

# CHAPTER 16
## ENOUGH IS ENOUGH

*Matthew 5:23-25 NIV[51]*
*23 "Therefore, if you are offering your gift at the altar and there remember that your brother or sister has something against you, 24 leave your gift there in front of the altar. First go and be reconciled to them; then come and offer your gift. 25 "Settle matters quickly with your adversary who is taking you to court. Do it while you are still together on the way, or your adversary may hand you over to the judge, and the judge may hand you over to the officer, and you may be thrown into prison.*

If there is one universal absolute that will need to take place in every marriage on an ongoing basis, it's **forgiveness.** This one thing stands above the rest and is a continual need, no matter how long you have been together or how many challenges and struggles you have faced before. You will need ongoing forgiveness to succeed.

In a Christian marriage, this concept is generally understood. The problem arises when one or both spouses reach a point where they can *forgive no more*. It is in these moments that I, as a marriage counselor, have often found myself walking with couples. Whether it is infidelity issues, irreparable financial choices, or just the continual deception that one spouse continues to engage in, forgiveness is the core issue.

A couple came into my office one day for a counseling appointment. By all external measures, anyone would have thought this was a marriage made in heaven. I honestly did not even realize they had set up the appointment for assistance in their marriage. I thought it was to pray for them over some extraneous situation or business transaction. I soon learned that they had reached a spot in their marriage that, for one of them, was an unforgivable and impassable situation. They sat on opposite sides of my office, hands folded tightly in their laps, and acted very cold to one another. As is my custom, I opened in prayer and then asked them what I could do to assist them.

Finally, after a long period of silence, the wife took a deep breath and said, "Pastor, I am the problem. I have never once cheated on my husband physically. But for whatever reason, I cannot stop my flirtatious activities with other men. For a long time, I thought it was just a teenage habit that I needed to break. But over time, I realized that it was way deeper and more sinister than that. It was something that had become so habitual that, many times, I was doing it without even realizing it. Unfortunately, many of those times have been directly in front of my husband, the man I love, without even being cognizant of what I was doing. So many times, he would walk away in disgust and embarrassment over my comments or my lewdness with a stranger. I am so embarrassed. But he has informed me due to my last indiscretion with this that he has no trust for me, believes I will never stop, and he cannot continue to live with this behavior."

It was at this moment that I proceeded to ask a few questions. No. 1: How long have you been married? (The answer was twenty-seven years.) No. 2: How long has this problem been visible and unchecked? The husband spoke up for the first time. (Twenty-eight years.) That's when I realized we were in for a long haul.

The first thing that I suggested was for her to go through a ministry of deliverance from demonic bondage, because evidently, there was something that was spiritually attached to her. I knew this by the way she described engaging in this flirtatious activity without willfully or consciously deciding to do it beforehand. I then turned to her husband and requested that he wait to see what could be done over the next six months before he went through with separation or divorce. He agreed to this, saying that she was the love of his life and the only person he's ever wanted. However, the strain of being continually emotionally abused and rejected had brought him to his breaking point. His biggest problem with the whole situation was that his wife had stopped flirting with him years ago. This communicated to him that she thought he was not good enough for her.

After weeks of counseling and a very powerful deliverance for this woman, we were able to stand together in the sanctuary of the church on a beautiful Friday morning and renew their vows. I am proud to say that was almost fourteen years ago. They are still married to this day, and theirs is one of the most powerful marriages I have ever seen. What I left out is all the stuff in the middle that happened with him crying and sobbing repeatedly again about how much rejection and self-image issues this had created in his life. With forgiveness issues, no matter what the wrong that has happened, both people end up holding resentment, animosity, and hurt. That's why forgiveness is a daily, sometimes hourly, process within any marriage. In order for marriage to be healthy, whole, and vibrant, this must be the case. No committed marital relationship is going to function or endure without forgiveness. If you are saving hurtful issues for later to use against your spouse, you are walking in unforgiveness.

What are the things you are holding onto that you haven't truly forgiven? Why? Is there broken trust? Perhaps there is a continuation of old behaviors in your spouse that you had hoped would be dealt with by now. Are there past hurts, either from your spouse or from people in your past? Is there retelling of toxic narratives that bring dishonor, or uncover vulnerable places in your heart with the one who was supposed to protect you most?

What does real forgiveness look like? Maybe you have tried to forgive in the past, but those feelings of hurt keep coming to the surface again and again, reminding you of what the other person did or said. Are there marked moments in time that you will *never* forgive and *never* let go of? Those are the dangerous ones. You can only bury and avoid them for so long before they come to the surface, where they must be dealt with.

Can I tell you something? You will often end up getting what you fear. You get the byproduct of what you fear when you dwell on that fear. You must not allow yourself to continue in unforgiveness or jealousy. Instead, you must willfully choose forgiveness for the benefit of you and your spouse.

I once did a series of counseling sessions with a couple that had been married for about five years. The woman had been in a serious relationship with a man before meeting her husband. She had broken off all ties with her ex-boyfriend before her wedding day. But on the day of her wedding, she got a text from her ex, pouring his heart out to her and saying he still loved her. She had not talked to this person in months. Then on the day of her wedding, he decided to jump in and cause chaos.

To make matters worse, she was not the first to see the text message. Her brand new husband-to-be was actually the one who picked up her phone and read it. When he saw it, there was a massive confrontation that escalated at the back of the church. It is one of the only times that, minutes before a couple was about to be married, I had to go into an intensive counseling session. She reassured him that there had been no communication, and she proved it with the timestamps on her phone. She immediately blocked her ex and proclaimed her undying loyalty and faithfulness to her fiancé. After this, they were able to have an amazing, healing moment. But it was only for a moment.

The damage was done, and she had no idea just how bad it was going to get. She tried to reassure her new husband that he had nothing to worry about. She did not even answer the text and was never going to see this person again. But the husband was, understandably, upset. As they set off on their honeymoon, they had a dark cloud hanging over them. As she sat in that counseling session five years later, she told me that it had ruined their honeymoon.

All the while, her husband sat beside her on the small couch in my office, arms crossed over his chest. He said very little during the first part of the session. The wife went on to tell me that they had tried to work out this circumstance, and she thought that it had all been taken care of on their wedding day. There were times when things were good, and her husband would not bring this incident up. But there were other times it was his go-to dig in order to guilt-trip and manipulate her. He would accuse her of not really loving him. Anytime they had a fight, her husband brought up this situation with her ex texting her on their wedding day—a situation that was completely out of her control. She didn't ask that man to text her. She hadn't even talked to this other person in months before the wedding. However, every time they had a point of conflict come up in their marriage, her husband used this as a weapon against her.

It had gotten to the point that things were so bad between them that she was contemplating divorce. She was thinking of leaving him because of it. But she also knew that the Bible taught against divorce, which is why they had come to see me before they progressed into separation. Tearfully, she said to me, "Pastor, I want to make this marriage work. I genuinely love my husband. But I can't seem to do anything right. I can't seem to do anything to pay for this person texting me on our wedding day. I can't do this anymore. I am so tired of living under the guilt of something I had no control over."

I thanked her for being vulnerable in telling me what was going on. I then turned to the husband, still stewing on his side of the couch. I looked him right in the eye and asked him, "So, you're holding this against your wife. How is that going for you?"

He got very heated and said, "Well, if she wants some other guy, then I don't see how we can make this marriage work!"

After thinking for a moment, I said, "Do you realize your bitterness and unforgiveness are going to cause exactly what you're afraid of?" The husband said nothing, but I could see that it had hit a nerve. "You are so afraid that your wife is going to cheat on you, that you are going to drive her to do just that. She is at her breaking point, and eventually, she is going to leave you. Is this really what you want?"

I would love to give you a great fairytale ending to this story. But I cannot. Over the course of the next six to eight months, there was a pause in his continual insecurity over this incident and his overwhelming fear of his wife cheating on him. Unfortunately, he fell right back into the same guilt and manipulation practices he had engaged in that had brought them into my office in the first place. As a result, she finally did what she told him she was going to do, and they got a divorce.

## Marriage Takes Trust

Marriage involves a commitment to provide and protect. There must be safety in marriage, or it will dissolve into chaos. If you genuinely cannot trust your spouse, there must be a serious evaluation of your heart. The persons involved must realize this responsibility before entering into the state of matrimony. The Bible warns those who fail to take care of their family with the following verse:

> *I Timothy 5:8 NIV[52]*
> *8 But if anyone does not provide for his own, and especially for those of his household, he has denied the faith and is worse than an unbeliever.*

Part of taking care of your family involves doing the hard things to ensure a successful relationship. It's time to root out the conflict.

### 1. What is the Source of Quarrels and Conflicts Among You?

It's selfishness and stubbornness that cause the vast majority of the conflict in your relationships, families, and marriages. When you become aware of something you did or said that was wrong, confess it. Forgive, forget, and move on. God doesn't want you to be miserable, wallowing in your failures. You need to see your spouse through the eyes God sees *you* with. Honestly, this is very simple to understand and grasp. How would you feel if every time you screwed up, God spent months or even years reminding you of how much you hurt Him? Praise the Lord, His forgiveness is exactly the kind I'm talking about right here. He doesn't want to use your sin as a way to create quarrels and conflicts between you and Him. He totally forgives and immediately forgets. Don't fall into the trap of feeling that because you're a human, and not God, that you have a right to do something other than the way He does something. Again, this is selfish and stubborn. I would like to quote a great and wonderful video sitcom, created by Bob Newhart, where he plays a psychiatrist. A young woman comes to him and has a series of ridiculous problems, including the fear of being buried alive in a box. He tells her the solution: *stop it*. She is appalled at his simple advice. She's convinced there has to be more to his solution. He then says, "Stop it, or I'll bury you alive in a box!" That is the best advice I could ever give a couple that continues to have contention over unforgiveness issues. Stop it!

Why does there always have to be a winner and a loser in marriage? Why can't we just both be winners? Stop keeping score and start being the keeper of your spouse's heart. *Keeping score* involves keeping your spouse at a distance. *Keeping their heart* means protecting them and bringing them closer. Women may love this paragraph because they naturally assume, by how it was written, that it is intended to motivate their husbands. The truth is, it was written for both of you. The issue with conflict and quarreling is people make a different set of rules for themselves than they do for their spouse, assuming it's the other person who needs to be fixed. Both partners must have a soft heart.

The following verses of scripture illustrate Jesus' perspective (which is ultimately God's perspective) on what real forgiveness looks like:

*Matthew 18:21-35 NKJV*[53]
*21 Then Peter came to Him and said, "Lord, how often shall my brother sin against me, and I forgive him? Up to seven times?" 22 Jesus said to him, "I do not say to you, up to seven times, but up to seventy times seven. 23 Therefore the kingdom of heaven is like a certain king who wanted to settle accounts with his servants. 24 And when he had begun to settle accounts, one was brought to him who owed him ten thousand talents. 25 But as he was not able to pay, his master commanded that he be sold, with his wife and children and all that he had, and that payment be made. 26 The servant therefore fell down before him, saying, 'Master, have patience with me, and I will pay you all.' 27 Then the master of that servant was moved with compassion, released him, and forgave him the debt. 28 "But that servant went out and found one of his fellow servants who owed him a hundred denarii; and he laid hands on him and took him by the throat, saying, 'Pay me what you owe!' 29 So his fellow servant fell down at his feet and begged him, saying, 'Have patience with me, and I will pay you all.' 30 And he would not, but went and threw him into prison till he should pay the debt. 31 So when his fellow servants saw what had been done, they were very grieved, and came and told their master all that had been done. 32 Then his master, after he had called him, said to him, 'You wicked servant! I forgave you all that debt because you begged me. 33 Should you not also have had com-*

*passion on your fellow servant, just as I had pity on you?' **34** And his master was angry, and delivered him to the torturers until he should pay all that was due to him. **35** "So My heavenly Father also will do to you if each of you, from his heart, does not forgive his brother his trespasses."*

After reading these verses of scripture, can you honestly say that this is the way you practice forgiveness in your marriage every single time? If you do not forgive, God, your Heavenly Father, cannot forgive you. Not only that, you are putting yourself in a world of torment until you choose to *forgive*.

## MARRIAGE ACTIVATION 16

Unforgiveness is a prison of your own making. The Word says that God cannot forgive you if you do not forgive others (Matthew 6:14-15). That is a scary place to be! We must purpose to root out all unforgiveness in our hearts in order to move forward into all that God has for us.

1. Is there bitterness and unforgiveness in your heart that you have been holding against your spouse? Past wounds are not a badge of honor. They are killing your marriage like a cancer from the inside out. Take some time now to confess any unforgiveness that you have been holding in your heart—whether against your spouse or any person in your life. (This could be a parent, or someone from your past that you have not been able to forgive.) Do that now in a

moment of vulnerability and safety with your spouse.
2. Now, I want you to hold hands and *release* forgiveness. I want you to let them know that they are forgiven and loved, thank them for sharing what they did, and then vow to put those things behind you. It says in Psalm 103:12 that God does not remember our sins. They are as far as the east is from the west. If He does not remember our sins against Him, how much more should we not hold our spouses' sins against them?
3. Pray together and seal this moment. I want you to continue to hold hands and pray over each other and promise to move on with forgiveness and kindness.

# CHAPTER 17

## HOW MANY ARE IN OUR BED?

I could feel the spirit of shame and guilt as soon as they walked into my office. It is not uncommon for me to feel things in the spirit realm before anyone says a word as couples come into the counseling session. My heart broke when the atmosphere was suddenly saturated by the heaviness that this couple was carrying. We prayed to get started, and then I asked them to tell me what was going on.

The husband started, hesitantly at first, but then grew more passionate as he let out his frustration. "Pastor, we got married a few months ago, and I will say, we did make our mistakes before we got married. We've repented of that season and were abstinent before the wedding. I'm gonna be honest, she didn't seem nervous about anything I asked her to do before we chose to do it the right way. But now that we're married, she doesn't seem to want to do *anything*."

The wife shifted uncomfortably, and I knew this was

going to be a difficult subject for her to open up about. I turned to her and asked her, "Would you agree with your husband on his explanation?"

She wouldn't even look me in the eyes. "Yes, I suppose so," she mumbled.

"And how do you feel about the intimacy you share in your marriage?" I asked.

Tears started streaming down her face. "Pastor, I know this sounds crazy, but now that we are married, I just can't see myself doing those things with him anymore as his wife. It feels...dirty."

You could have heard a pin drop in that room. I allowed the silence for a moment, then went on. "So you were okay with having sex provocatively and exotically before marriage, specifically before you and your husband came to Christ, but now you think sex is dirty?"

"Yes," she replied. "I just can't seem to get all the bad things I did in my past out of my mind. I can't get away from that feeling of guilt anytime we even think about being intimate with each other." She seemed to be closing in on herself before my eyes.

"This is what it sounds like you are saying to me: you feel you have to punish yourself and your current spouse for the mistakes you made in your past. You think that this will absolve you of all the guilt and memories the enemy keeps placing on you from all of those past exploits? It seems to me you seem to think you have not adequately punished yourself for what you did with past partners and each other. Would you say that's correct?"

She nodded, but again wouldn't look at me or her spouse.

"Do you realize that your attempt to punish yourself is also punishing the man that you fell in love with and longed to make your husband?" I pressed.

She did look at me then, and I could tell by the horror on her face that that was the last thing she had intended. She looked at her husband, and he grabbed her hand. "No, I'm not trying to punish him. It's my fault—" she trailed off, but I could see the questions and realization were starting to click. She had indeed been overwhelmed by shame and guilt because of other people being in her head and her bed when she tried to make love to her husband.

"Without realizing it, you have been punishing him for the things you did in your past, the things you did apart from him, and then the things you did when you got together before you started to do things the right way. If you refuse to forgive yourself, you are going to keep allowing those sins to bring division and destruction into your relationship and, most importantly, into your marriage. You are going to keep yourself from being intimate with him—in ways that are not sinful in the eyes of God—even when it is perfectly acceptable and good for you to do them now. You are believing a lie of the enemy over the joy of your intimacy with your husband."

She continued to cry, but I could see we were starting to make a breakthrough. I looked at both of them and said, "You've got too many people in your bed." They looked at me as if I were crazy. Then they both assured me that they were not cheating on each other, and they were not swingers.

I shook my head. "I know that without a doubt. What I mean is that every time you come together, you allow the enemy to throw a memory back in your face. You come under guilt and shame. You can't seem to be intimate in the way you want to with your husband because the emotions or memories you associate with those different acts in your past come flying back to the forefront of your mind."

She nodded vigorously, and her eyes got wide. "Yeah, that's exactly what's happening!" She looked at her husband and gripped his hand even tighter. "I don't want anyone to come between us, so I feel like it's better not to be intimate in the ways he wants than to see someone else in my mind."

I said, "The first step for overcoming this is to have true repentance over these situations. You have already turned away from doing the things you used to do with the people you used to be with, correct?"

They both answered that they were doing things God's way.

I said, "Good. Then the second step is forgiveness. The kind of forgiveness I'm talking about is not external, it's internal." I looked at the wife until she met my gaze. "You have to forgive *yourself*."

## Who's Been Sleeping in My Bed?

This story all comes down to *soul ties*. As we've discussed in the chapters on covenant, there is a physical bond that happens between a man and woman when they come together sexually for the first time. It was meant to be a blood covenant that bound them together physically, but also emotionally and spiritually. This is often referred to as a soul tie. When the Bible says that *"the two shall become one flesh...*" (Genesis 2:24), it wasn't just a figurative, abstract idea. It is a literal, physical, emotional, and spiritual truth. When you give yourself sexually to someone, you become one with that person. This happens with anyone that you choose to have sexual activity with (even a prostitute, a secret lover, or someone you may never even meet on your smartphone through pornography or illicit connections). That is why God designed sex to be the private, covenant act of marriage.

Unfortunately, many people give themselves away before marriage. All too often, they give themselves away to multiple partners. This is in no way meant to add shame and guilt to what may be a sordid past, but it is a reality for so many people. If we are going to experience freedom and purity along with beautiful sexual and emotional intimacy with our spouse (the way God designed it), then these issues must be addressed.

When a couple engages in sex, a hormone called dopamine is instantly released. God created this hormone for one reason, and that is so we would come back for more and more of it. This is the pleasure hormone, and it makes us want to repeat the act. It is a reward, so to speak. Hormones, such as oxytocin and vasopressin, are released during sexual intercourse. Women have more receptors for oxytocin, while men have more vasopressin receptors. But these are both hormones that emotionally attach us to someone. God created these receptors for a reason. He wanted sex to bond two people together in a way that would never happen with someone else. You are literally bonded with another person in the physiological makeup of your mind when you are sexually intimate with them.[54]

This is good in a marriage because sex was meant to bring pleasure and bond you with your spouse. God wanted married couples to re-engage in sexual and emotional intimacy so they would stay together in those bonds, and create babies for the furthering of the human race *and* His kingdom.

However, it is not good outside of marriage. When you have multiple partners, a piece of you remains with them forever, and you are connected with them for the rest of your life (thus a soul tie has been made). The more people you connect (and then disconnect) with, the weaker your receptors become for those hormones. That is why people who have had multiple partners before marriage are more likely to get divorced. Their connection receptors are weakened and broken more easily, thus defeating the purpose of why God created them in the first place—so they would be used with one person on your wedding night and then forever more.

## How Long Will You Allow the Past to Dictate Your Future?

Most sexual flings for a male are not emotional. They are driven by a physical need for release.

Females, on the other hand, remember everything. They tend to form stronger emotional attachments. Now, does this make men the devil? No. It makes them different. Most of the intimacy issues I see in counseling that are connected to soul ties are in women, obviously because of their deeper emotional response and surrender to the sex act. Women remember past sexual encounters in vivid detail: what her partner smelled like, what music was playing in the background, and the emotions and thoughts that were going through her mind at the exact time of the encounter. And it is most often women who live with the overwhelming guilt, because they were created to have not only a physical attachment with their spouse, but an emotional and spiritual one as well. Men have these responses as well, but they can manifest differently. Regardless, the emotional weight that is carried over from past encounters can create serious divisions in marriage.

It is so important to deal with these soul ties so the enemy will not be able to keep you distant and cold. If you continue to punish each other over past experiences, choices, and even the mental and emotional scarring that took place, you will continue to be trapped in an exhausting cycle of brokenness. There must be forgiveness, for your partner and yourself, if you are to move forward in being your best self with your *covenant spouse*. God designed you to be sexually active with one another on a continual basis. That was His divine plan.

## Breaking Soul Ties

Soul ties from past sexual exploits are a form of demonic oppression. They are blockades and weights that Satan loves to put on people so they remain stuck in a cycle of guilt and shame. He also does this so they remain ineffective for the Kingdom of God. If the enemy can slowly chip away at your marriage, he can chip away at the family unit. If the enemy is successful in doing this, he will be able to cause even more havoc and chaos. Don't let him do it.

There are many reading this book who are carrying a load of sexual baggage already. You wish you could go back and do things differently. You would love to know the kind of intimacy that God originally had in mind for husbands and wives—but you feel it's too late. God is all about redeeming things that are lost that the enemy has tried to steal, kill, and destroy. That's why in John 10:10, He says, *"I have come to give them life more abundantly."* He wants to redeem His people and His creation. In fact, here are four steps to redeeming your sex life:

1. **Repentant Hearts.**

What does that mean? It means to change your mind. It means that you agree with God, that He is right, and you were wrong. Repentance means that you get yourself in line with God's standards *today*. Not next week. Not eventually. Your past is over today. Whatever it was in your past (and your present) that is still partnering with unrighteousness and unholiness needs to be confessed immediately. Whether it's past memories, current sexual temptations, or even self-indulging pleasure, it has to end today. It's time to repent and allow God to heal you so you can give all of yourself to the spouse He gave you.

2. **Receive Forgiveness.**

God is waiting to forgive, cleanse, and restore you. You can be released from the shame and guilt of past failures. Probably the heaviest load any of us carries is the load of guilt for our sins. I would venture to say that a lot of that guilt surrounds sexual sins. *Let it go.* God wants to forgive you. But you need to ask for and receive His forgiveness. *If you ever want to have true intimacy with your spouse, you must first have intimacy with God.*

### 3. Refocused Thoughts.

This is where it gets really tough. We need to turn our backs on the sexual things that invade our minds. There is really only one way to do this. When those thoughts overwhelm, whatever they may be and however ugly and awful they are, you must take authority over them out loud so the enemy cannot torment you in the secret place of your mind. The minute you shine light on those thoughts (even in your embarrassment), the enemy always has to flee. James 4:7 NIV says, *"Resist the devil and he will flee from you."* [55] We need to get tough on our TV watching and the movies we watch. If you are unwilling to put that safety net in place on your computer to keep pornography from coming into your eyes, then you are *not* serious about this issue—that's just the honest truth. We need to refocus our minds on God's standard. That means fighting for purity in our entertainment, in our leisure, and especially in our minds and thoughts.

> *1 Thessalonians 4:3-7 NIV*[56]
> *3 It is God's will that you should be sanctified: that you should avoid sexual immorality; 4 that each of you should learn to control your own body in a way that is holy and honorable, 5 not in passionate lust like the pagans, who do not know God; 6 and that in this matter no*

*one should wrong or take advantage of a brother or sister. The Lord will punish all those who commit such sins, as we told you and warned you before. 7 For God did not call us to be impure, but to live a holy life.*

***Ephesians 5:3 NIV*[9]**
*3 "Among you there must not be even a hint of sexual immorality."*

We need to be making the tough decisions and the firm commitments to refocus our thoughts and deeds on God's standards.

4. **Request Help.**

Pornography is one of the biggest thieves, if not the biggest, in marital intimacy. If you struggle with pornography, I highly recommend the book *Every Man's Battle* if you are a man and *Every Woman's Battle* if you are a woman. Pornography is immensely dangerous because, just as in intimacy between a man and woman, dopamine is released when you are watching other people engage in sexual activity. It is this dopamine release that keeps you running back to porn. You are training yourself to be addicted to sexual activity aside from your spouse. You are stealing intimacy from your spouse. It is as powerful as a drug addiction: it *never* seems to be enough. Your brain keeps pressing you to get more of that dopamine high, and you have to go further and further down that rabbit hole, watching things you never even dreamed of, to get the same kind of dopamine release. There are some I have counseled who claim that at the height of their pornography addictions, they were watching 5-6 times a day and masturbating that many times to release. What does that leave for your spouse?

*Nothing.*

And that is where resentment kicks in. Your spouse may feel like they are no longer desirable to you, that they are not enough to satisfy you. You become distant because you feel guilty, and it leads to even more dysfunction in your marriage. You become roommates instead of lovers and partners.

I have counseled couples who feel they have to watch pornography before they can get turned on for one another. If this is truly the case, there is something desperately wrong. This is an area that needs to be brought forward as a couple and confessed to someone you don't want to confess it to (such as a counselor, pastor, or trusted friend) in order to be healed. That's the only way it will get broken, and you can create righteous, healthy, holy, pure, and new habits.

It is not just men who are struggling with porn addictions today. Twenty years ago, it was around a 90-10 rate, with men being the higher number. Now, it's more like 60-40. It presents differently for women. Romance or smutty novels are all the rage now. For women, this is just like watching porn because you are imagining the scenes in your mind. Trust me, through counseling many, many couples, I know this to be true. You must stop lying to yourself about it. These novels are geared to hit a woman in her heart and the emotional side of sex, but it is just as dangerous because it is taking your emotional energy and placing it on someone other than your husband—even if it's imaginary.

The bottom line is this: pornography is stealing from your marriage. Whether in video form or novels, it is stealing from your spouse until you no longer have the physical or emotional energy to give to them.

## What are the Boundaries?

I have talked with couples, especially older ones, who have been married for some time, and they wonder what is sin inside the bounds of marriage when it comes to sex. Are there certain positions they should not engage in, such as sodomy, oral sex, or sex toys?

I always ask them if they have prayed about it first.

I suggest that, if a couple is struggling with the idea of what is right or wrong for their marriage, they fast for a time and pray until they get an answer. Lock away the toys. Smash your computer or your smartphone if you have to, in order to guard your eyes from pornography. (Pornography is never okay in the marriage relationship, just to bring clarity once again.) Don't engage in a certain position that one or both of you are uncomfortable with. This doesn't mean forever, but until you both get the answers you are seeking from the Lord. When you have your answers from Jesus, then go forward with whatever He has told you is right and good in your marriage. Be careful not to take scripture out of its context because you need to read all around this verse to understand the overall context, but Paul says, the *marriage bed is undefiled (Hebrews 13:4)*. This is referenced to mean that anything and everything a couple finds mutually enjoyable and fun within the confines of their marriage covenant, absence of any conviction or scriptural instruction, God is saying, *"Go for it!"*

**Sexual Expectations Within Marriage**

Every single marriage, no matter how sexually active (or inactive) before the wedding day, has expectations that there will be similar or even better sexual encounters after the wedding day. This is where the problem arises—misaligned expectations. Usually, there will be some form of impasse that needs to be worked out after the wedding to get both parties' ideals and expectations on the same page. The following verse of scripture tells us God's expectation of our sexual expression:

> *Genesis 2:24 NIV*[1]
> *24 "Therefore a man shall leave his father and mother and be joined to his wife, and they shall become one flesh."*

From this verse of scripture, if you study it in its original form, *"they shall become one flesh"* does not mean a singular incident or time. It actually is referencing them becoming one flesh continually. Marriage is the beginning of a brand new family. And in every relationship, there are things that we need. Why has it become difficult for Christian couples to even admit that they have needs in the area of sexual fulfillment within their marriage? There is a thought process that is prevalent in Christian circles that we must lay everything down and just trudge through life without communicating what we need and desire from our spouses in the area of sex. That mindset is not only ridiculous but incredibly damaging.

We all have needs. It is not a bad thing. It's a part of life. But how we handle meeting and communicating those needs is what will make or break a marriage.

Why should you learn to understand, appreciate, and fulfill one another's physical and emotional needs? First, because you have an obligation biblically to do so. Paul says in I Corinthians 7:5[7], to *"not forsake the coming together of yourselves except for an agreed upon time for fasting and prayer,"* speaking specifically of sexual fulfillment. Your spouse has made a vow to meet these needs *only* in the bond of the marriage relationship. They have nowhere else to (legitimately) go. Second, because if you don't fulfill these needs, someone else may step in and take your place. That's just the truth. Not that this excuses adultery or makes the innocent party responsible. All of us are vulnerable to temptation. If you want to protect your mate from temptation, then you're going to have to step up and protect them by providing and meeting their sexual needs.

Why do husbands and wives often fail to meet their spouse's deepest needs?

The answer is at once simple and heartbreaking: selfishness and ignorance. Ignorance is the *inability to understand* and appreciate your spouse's individual needs and desires. Selfishness is an *unwillingness* to meet those needs and desires. One is a heart problem, and the other is a head problem. One can be solved by information, the other, only by repentance. But both must be addressed in order for the relationship to improve, heal, and grow past this failure.

Men and women have similar needs, but they rank them differently. That is because our brains are wired differently by God. It does not make one gender better or more spiritual than the other, with the other being more sexual and worldly.

We have already demonstrated this chart in a previous chapter, but we will once again use it here to convey the importance of understanding the needs of one gender versus another.

**Men**

1. Sexual fulfillment
2. Recreational companionship
3. An attractive spouse
4. Domestic support
5. Admiration

**Women**

1. Affection
2. Conversation
3. Honesty and openness
4. Financial support
5. Family commitment

As you can tell from this particular graph, sexual fulfillment is No. 1 for men, whereas on most charts, affection is

No. 1 for women. The reality is, they are actually the exact same thing, although the enemy has twisted it to make both parties feel there is a difference. Do not allow the enemy to continue stealing from you. Get any extra people out of your bed by walking through repentance, forgiveness, and vowing to meet one another's needs in the kindness and joy set forth by the Word of God.

# MARRIAGE ACTIVATION 17

God's desire is that we live in total freedom and restoration. He comes to not only save us from our sins, but set us free from the things that would try to keep us from abundant life. As you go through the activations this week, ask the Lord to bring health and renewed joy in your sexual relationship with your spouse.

## FREEDOM PRAYER:

Father, I thank You for Jesus and for my salvation through Him. He is my Savior, and I am the sinner. I am so grateful to be washed in His Blood, saved by His Grace, and set free by His Holy Spirit.
Because You have forgiven me, I choose to forgive everyone who has hurt me, lied to me, or disappointed me. I repent of anger, bitterness and hatred, of rebellion, resentment and revenge.

I repent of envy, jealousy and strife, of fear and lust, of doubt and unbelief, of witchcraft and idolatry, and of every work of the flesh. I denounce the sins of my ancestors and confess myself to be totally free from any and all ancestral curses.

I renounce all unholy vows, oaths, pledges, and ceremonies engaged in or made by myself, or by any of my ancestors.

I denounce and confess as sin all unholy soul ties and choose to be free from them.

I put everything under the Blood of Jesus, and by doing so, I break every stronghold of power in my life.

Jesus Christ is my Savior and Lord. He's my deliverer, my healer, and He broke the power of all curses. I choose to be free, and I will be free. By the *power* of the Holy Spirit, I am *free*.

In Jesus' name.

Amen*

1. Both of you separately pick one idea of what you can do to be intimate with the other one tonight. Do not tell your partner what that intimate activity is. Now it's time to flip a coin. Whoever wins, goes first. Share that intimate act and then take the next fifteen to twenty minutes

---

* This prayer was adapted and inspired with permission from Don Dickerman out of his book: Dickerman, D. (2009). *When Pigs Move in*. Charisma Media.

to fulfill it. Then, follow suit in the same way with the other intimate act.

2. This one is harder. Sit down and write three things you feel have been blockades that have stopped the fun and joy of your intimacy and sexual connection within your marriage. For the next week, I want you to privately pray over those three things multiple times in a day. At the end of the seventh day, I don't want you to say a word about them to your spouse. (Not one word). At this time, I want you to come together and trade lists. Now, for the next seven days (still not speaking about them) you pray over your spouses' list multiple times a day. Then at the end of fourteen days, come together to formulate a plan on how to start doing all of them.

# CHAPTER 18
## WHAT HAPPENED TO THE PASSION?

Sexual intimacy can be a difficult subject to broach, especially in the church. There can be a number of reasons for a lack in this area: medical conditions, tiredness, or not placing it in the right priority. Most often, it is a skewed mindset that brings destruction to healthy intimacy.

Listen to these poetic words:

*"The sweet, fragrant curves of your body, the soft, spiced contours of your flesh invite me, and I come. I stay until dawn breathes its light and night slips away. You're beautiful from head to toe, my dear love, beautiful beyond compare, absolutely flawless. You've captured my heart, dear friend. You looked at me, and I fell in love. One look my way and I was hopelessly in love! How beautiful your love, dear, dear friend - far more pleasing than a fine, rare wine, your fragrance more exotic than select spices. The kisses of your lips are honey, my love,*

*every syllable you speak a delicacy to savor. Your clothes smell like the wild outdoors, the ozone scent of high mountains. Dear lover and friend, you're a secret garden, a private and pure fountain. Body and soul, you are paradise, a whole orchard of succulent fruits."*[57]

Wow! Who wrote such poetry? Keats? Byron? Shakespeare? No—those words of passionate sexuality were written by God. They were written by King Solomon, inspired by God Himself, to be included in His book—the Bible. You may have guessed, this portion of scripture is from the Song of Solomon. And yes, God included it in the Bible for a reason. God does not look on marital sex as a sin. He looks at it as something good. In fact, God created sex and proclaimed that it is *good*.

You want to know what the best sex in all of creation was? It was the sexual relationship that Adam and Eve had when God first created it, and they were enjoying it as it was meant to be, in complete wholeness and perfection, before sin entered the picture. Look at Genesis chapter 2, the last verse.

> *Genesis 2:25 NIV*[1]
> *"Adam and his wife were both naked, and they felt no shame."*

I believe that verse is loaded with meaning. Adam and Eve were able to enjoy their sexual relationship in the way that God originally had in mind for all of us. They were completely open with one another. There was no deceit, no masks, no hiding, no game-playing, no manipulation: just passionate love and sex. (Probably lots of sex.) There was no shame.

Their sexuality was not loaded down with the baggage of past sin, previous mistakes, or wrong selfish motives.

It is more than a coincidence that the first thing that happened after Adam and Eve sinned was that they realized they were naked. It's because the first thing Satan attacked after he got them into his lair of deception was their intimacy and vulnerability. The first dysfunction in the human race as a result of sin was a dysfunction in the sexual relationship between the husband and his wife. Isn't that frustrating for all of us who want to be healthy in our sex lives? Satan has been picking on it from the beginning. They realized they were naked, and they immediately sewed coverings together. Contrast that with *"and they felt no shame"* from Genesis 2:25. Now they were full of shame, and they began to hide from each other. When sin entered the picture, the intimacy between husband and wife was the first casualty. The coverings they made to hide themselves went far beyond their bodies—they began to hide themselves emotionally and spiritually from each other and from God. Isn't it ironic that so many people are still doing that today over the exact same stuff?

Our attempts at covering sin were not good enough. Anytime we try to cover sin in our own power (Adam and Eve's fig leaves), we'll come up short. The next thing God did was to make them a covering that was suitable: a blood sacrifice. The Word says He killed an animal and made skins for them to cover their nakedness.

Sin had to be paid for by blood, and God set that up after the Fall of Man. The Bible is all about redemption.

When Man fell, we were separated from God by our sins. But God had a plan to redeem us, to recapture us for Himself, by the Blood of the Perfect Lamb, the Son of God. It's through faith in Jesus Christ, and Him alone, that we can be saved and redeemed. Just as God has laid out a plan in His word to reconcile humanity to Himself, He has also laid out a plan for us to redeem sex—to make it *great* again. God had made the sexual desire very strong in humans, and so in His Word, He gave us some guidelines for great sex.

Hollywood would like to have us believe that the best sex is the passionate, animalistic, spur-of-the-moment sex between strangers, co-workers, neighbors, classmates, or friends. But study after study shows that the people who are most satisfied with their sex lives are monogamous husbands and wives. Yeah, that's right—*married people*. In fact, the highest levels of sexual satisfaction are experienced by married, evangelical Christians. The 1994 University of Chicago study, *Sex in America: The Definitive Survey*, found that monogamous conservative Christians reported the most physical satisfaction from sex. Several other studies show that married couples who attend church at least once a week are the most sexually contented segment of society. The last time I checked, the University of Chicago was decidedly not a Christian institution.

Why is it that Christians, of all people, are statistically proven to have healthier and better sex lives? Why is it that sex between married, evangelical Christians has the highest level of satisfaction in the country? Because they are doing sex *God's way*. You see, if God created sex, then it stands to reason that He is going to give the best instruction on sex—not the cast of FRIENDS, the author of *Fifty Shades of Grey*, or even Dr. Phil. The best advice about sex comes from God's Word.

Here are a couple of truths God teaches about sex:

1. **Sex with your spouse is supposed to be a regular, enjoyable part of your relationship.**

Proverbs 5:18 & 19 NIV[58] says, *"May your fountain be blessed, and may you rejoice in the wife of your youth...may her breasts satisfy you always, may you ever be captivated by her love."* Hey, guess what? We are to be satisfied by our lover. We are to rejoice in our wives and husbands, and we are to be captivated by their love for our entire lives. That is a biblical principle.

In I Corinthians 7:4-5 NIV[7], Paul says that husbands and wives have a responsibility to mutually love and satisfy each other's God-given sexual needs. He says, *"The husband should fulfill his marital duty to his wife, and likewise the wife to her husband. The wife's body does not belong to her alone but also to her husband, in the same way, the husband's body does not belong to him alone, but also to his wife."*

2. **Sexual harmony is found when each partner recognizes that they are giving and receiving a gift from one another and from God when they are intimate with one another.**

Sex is never about taking, conquering, or coercing. It is about giving, receiving, and mutually satisfying one another.

Those verses in 1 Corinthians bring up another point. You see where it says our bodies do not belong to us alone, but to our partner? That means that we have no right to be using our bodies for selfish reasons, manipulation, or guilt trips. When we pollute our body or our mind with unhealthy images or practices, or give that body to another, we are ignoring God's directions. That will weaken our sexual relationship with our spouse.

If you have sex with a person, any person outside of the bonds of marriage, you are hurting them, yourself, and your relationship with God. There is no room for maneuvering here. Sexual intimacy outside of marriage is *sin,* and that includes non-physical emotional adultery, sexual fantasy, masturbation, and cohabitation.

3. **There is no such thing as a victimless sexual sin.**

The Bible says, *"Do not be fooled, God will not be mocked—whatever you sow, you will reap the consequences."* (Galatians 6:7-8) Husbands and wives, the sexual activities that you partake in counter to God's directions will hurt you and your partner. This includes the emotional affair with the person at work, the continual, seemingly innocent, flirtatious behavior that sparks thoughts and fantasies not directed at your spouse. It includes the addiction to pornography on the internet or on the television, or even an inappropriate thought life. All of this will infect and deteriorate your relationship with your spouse. You may say that you've never cheated on your husband or wife. However, Jesus said, *"Whoever looks on a woman with lust after her in his heart has already committed adultery."* You may have never cheated on your spouse physically, but what have you *cheated them out of*? Have you cheated them out of your full attention, your full devotion, your full faithfulness, your pure sexual passion and hunger? Hebrews 13:4 NIV says, *"Marriage should be honored by all, and the marriage bed kept pure, for God will judge the adulterer and all the sexually immoral."*[59]

There are some major surprises that would await most Christians who may not understand all the graphic illustrations and sexual imagery within God's word. God details very explicitly His desire for our sexual connections within the bond of marriage.

## Make Each Other's Dreams Come True

God desires for His children in the bonds of marriage to enjoy coming into a sexual union that brings gratification, delight, and contentment to that marriage. That is the thing that He is desiring for us to strive for, and these things are also the things Satan is trying to erode and destroy with intimate sexual encounters outside of your marriage. You cannot have true gratification, true delight, and true contentment when you are not choosing to be intimate with your covenant spouse, God's way.

## MARRIAGE ACTIVATION 18

Holy passion between spouses is not only allowed, it is encouraged. This week's activation is all about reigniting the spark between you and your spouse.

1. What were the ways you were able to allow yourself to be sexually passionate with your spouse when you first got married that may have since flown away, maybe since you've had children or for some other reason?
2. Bring that back. The reason can be raw laziness and selfishness that these things have waned. The kids cannot control your world. They are in this world because of your original passion. Get that passion back.

This is your activity this week. Both of you write down two memories of something that you did as a couple that was out-of-the-box in your sexual intimacy before the kids came. Next, go to dinner, and tell each other those memories.

# LET'S MAKE A DEAL

It has been an honor to bring this resource to you. I pray that this book has brought clarity and revelation to what God intended marriage to be from the beginning, starting in the Garden of Eden. If you have participated in the Defraudment Clause or allowed your heart to grow cold or lazy with the never-ceasing tide of responsibility placed on your shoulders, it is time to ask the Lord for strength as you walk through the process of change. Either way, I pray that this material has rekindled the fire in you to go after your spouse's heart with all of yours.

There is one last story I want to share before we close. Mike and Sarah's story is one that may be all too familiar for so many couples. They were at the bank across the street from our church, trying to work out how they were going to split their bank account prior to their impending separation. They had an envelope of divorce papers in their truck, ready to go turn in at the courthouse. As they came back to their truck, they had yet another argument, thanks to the frustrations of what it would take to separate their finances and bank accounts after the divorce.

It was at that point that Mike looked out his window and saw our church right across the street. He looked over at Sarah and suggested that they try one last thing before they turned in the divorce papers. She snapped at him and said that she had begged him to go to counseling with her at a church, but he had refused. Mike nodded and realized that he had been bucking the tide as far as getting Christian counseling for most of their marriage. However, he was ready to try God's way before they made things final.

They walked across the street and came into the church offices. I could hear them talking with my receptionist and I went to the front foyer to see if I could help them. They detailed a little of the situation to me and we went to visit in my office for a few minutes. A lot of blaming and frustration was laid out over the next half-hour, and I let them vent everything to me that had caused such a breach between them. After a while, I held up my hand and said, "I know how to fix this."

They were very interested, and I told them to follow me. We walked into the sanctuary of the church, and I turned on one light. I had them come to the altar, and I had each of them kneel down on opposite sides of the aisle. "Each of you needs to pray and repent for the next few minutes. The main reason you two are having marital problems is because you have drifted away from God." They had told me this during their venting that they had both stopped making God a priority in their lives, and this is why they were having so many problems.

"You need to repent for not making God the center of

your marriage and family. Without Him, nothing I say or do is going to help keep you from filing those divorce papers."

I told them that I would sit in the back of the sanctuary and wait while they took the next few minutes to pray. After about three minutes, I could hear both of them crying as they poured out their hearts to God. Then, Mike got up and went across the aisle to where Sarah knelt at the altar and began to pray for her. Sarah's sobs became even louder. I walked down to the altar, and they got up, wiping at their tears.

"We've been married for twenty-seven years, and you've never prayed for me before. Not one time," Sarah said.

Mike said that was going to change from this day forward.

After that powerful time, I told them that I would hang on to the divorce papers in one of my filing cabinets, and I would see them over the course of the next six weeks. Mike and Sarah started attending our church, and God did a miracle in their marriage during that time.

Before the second-to-last marriage counseling session, I set the envelope out on the edge of my desk. When they walked in, they both gave the envelope the side-eye as they sat down. I could see throughout the first few minutes of this session that it was making both of them uncomfortable, but I kept on as if nothing was amiss.

Finally, after they had glared at that envelope several times, I said, "You guys are really annoyed by that, aren't you?"

Sarah immediately piped up and said, "Yes, Pastor! It's like it's trespassing. I can't believe we were that close to filing those papers. I don't want to look at them ever again."

I handed the envelope to Mike, and he held it away from him like it was a dead fish. I told them that they had to get the D-word out of their vocabulary from that day forward. "Divorce cannot be an option anymore. Or else, when hard times come again, and they will, you guys will be right back where you started when we first met."

I encouraged them to get alone that weekend, so they decided to go to the beach and have a second honeymoon. While they were there, they sent me a video of them having a bonfire on the beach and throwing the divorce papers into the flames. Then, they roasted marshmallows over the fire. They had a great time for the rest of the weekend, recommitting their lives to one another, growing closer to each other, and allowing God to grow closer to them as they planned a fresh start.

This is what it takes to make a great marriage. This beautiful story of reconciliation and what God can do to heal and restore a marriage. It can be your story as well. Let's make a deal, right here and now. Get the word *divorce* out of your vocabulary. Commit that it is not, and never will be, an option.

Commit today, moving forward, to communicate with your spouse in healthy ways, to be the teammate, best friend, and lover that you set out to be at the beginning of your marriage. Recommit to your spouse. And if needed, come back to these pages and the things that you have written down about your marriage when you face hard times in the future.

Saying, "I do" in the beginning is wonderful. Even after

all the hard times, all the difficulties, and all the nuances of marriage, choose to let those three simple words be your anthem, "I *still* do". It's time not only to strive for your marriage, but to thrive in it. Make a deal with yourself, your spouse, and with God, to not only be a reader of His Word, but a *doer* of it. Put action to what you have read through this resource, and I promise you, you will see real, lasting change come into your marriage. Watch your relationship blossom and thrive. I bless you in the name of Jesus.

# FURTHER READING

**Books:**

- *The 5 Love Languages - The secret to Love that Lasts* by Gary Chapman
- *Communication: Key to your Marriage* by H. Norma Wright
- *If Only He Knew: A Valuable Guide to Knowing, Understanding, and Loving Your Wife* by Gary Smalley
- *Every Man's Battle* by Stephen Arterburn, Fred Stoeker, Mike Yorkey
- *Every Woman's Battle* by Shannon Ethridge and Stephen Arterburn

# Podcasts and Marriage Apps:

- *Ultimate Intimacy* App
- *Ultimate Intimacy Podcast* by Nick and Amy

# A NOTE FROM THE AUTHOR

Thank you so much for reading *I Still Do*. I pray that it has helped to bring lasting change, peace, and restoration in your marriage. I am incredibly honored and proud of all the work you and your spouse have done. Please know from the bottom of my heart that I and my team here at Refuge City Church are praying for you.

If *I Still Do* has impacted your life, please consider leaving an Amazon review, and purchase a few more copies to give away to others who would benefit.* This will help *I Still Do* reach more people with the restorative power of God for their marriages.

Continue to press forward in all that God has for you as a couple.

*Philippians 1:6 ESV[60]*
*6 And I am sure of this, that he who began a good work in you will bring it to completion at the day of Jesus Christ.*

Much love in Christ,
James Boyd

---

* Amazon Review Link: https://a.co/d/h76XBhu

# RESOURCES

1. *Genesis 2:18; 20b-25 (NIV)*. (n.d.-b). Bible Gateway. https://www.biblegateway.com/passage/?search=Genesis%202%3A18%3B%2020-25&version=NIV
2. *1 John 4:15-19 (NIV)*. (n.d.). Bible Gateway. https://www.biblegateway.com/passage/?search=1%20John%204%3A15-19&version=NIV
3. *Luke 14:25-34 (NIV)*. (n.d.). Bible Gateway. https://www.biblegateway.com/passage/?search=Luke%2014%3A25-34&version=NIV
4. *Proverbs 27:17 (NIV)*. (n.d.-b). Bible Gateway. https://www.biblegateway.com/passage/?search=Proverbs%2027%3A17&version=NIV
5. *John 13:1-17 (NIV)*. (n.d.). Bible Gateway. https://www.biblegateway.com/passage/?search=John%2013%3A%201-17&version=NIV
6. *2 Corinthians 5:14-21 (NIV)*. (n.d.). Bible Gateway. https://www.biblegateway.com/passage/?search=2%20Corinthians%205%3A14-21&version=NIV
7. *1 Corinthians 7:4-5; 12-16 (NIV)*. (n.d.). Bible Gateway. https://www.biblegateway.com/passage/?search=1%20Corinthians%207%3A12-16&version=NIV
8. *Philippians 1:3-6 (NIV)*. (n.d.). Bible Gateway. https://www.biblegateway.com/passage/?search=Philippians%201%3A3-6&version=NIV
9. *Ephesians 5:3; 22-29 (NIV)*. (n.d.). Bible Gateway. https://www.biblegateway.com/passage/?search=Ephesians%205%3A28-29&version=NIV
10. *Matthew 19:1-9 (NIV)*. (n.d.). Bible Gateway. https://www.biblegateway.com/passage/?search=Matthew%2019%3A7-8&version=NIV

11. *1 Peter 3:1-7 (NIV)*. (n.d.). Bible Gateway. https://www.biblegateway.com/passage/?search=1%20Peter%203%3A7&version=NIV
12. covenant. (2025). In *Merriam-Webster Dictionary*. https://www.merriam-webster.com/dictionary/covenant#:~:text=%3A%20a%20written%20agreement%20or%20promise,breach%20of%20such%20a%20contract
13. *Ecclesiastes 4:9-12 (NIV)*. (n.d.). Bible Gateway. https://www.biblegateway.com/passage/?search=Ecclesiastes%204%3A9-12&version=NIV
14. *Ephesians 4:29 (NKJV)*. (n.d.). Bible Gateway. https://www.biblegateway.com/passage/?search=Ephesians%204%3A29&version=NKJV
15. *Proverbs 17:1 (NIV)*. (n.d.). Bible Gateway. https://www.biblegateway.com/passage/?search=Proverbs%2017%3A1&version=NIV
16. *Proverbs 16:24 (NIV)*. (n.d.). Bible Gateway. https://www.biblegateway.com/passage/?search=Proverbs%2016%3A24&version=NIV
17. *James 1:19 (NIV)*. (n.d.). Bible Gateway. https://www.biblegateway.com/passage/?search=James%201%3A19&version=NIV
18. *Proverbs 13:3 (NIV)*. (n.d.). Bible Gateway. https://www.biblegateway.com/passage/?search=Proverbs%2013%3A3&version=NIV
19. *Matthew 5:37 (NIV)*. (n.d.). Bible Gateway. https://www.biblegateway.com/passage/?search=Matthew%205%3A37&version=NIV
20. *Revelation 19:6-9 (ESV)*. (n.d.). Bible Gateway. https://www.biblegateway.com/passage/?search=Revelation%2019%3A6-9&version=ESV
21. *Jeremiah 33:10-11 (NIV)*. (n.d.-b). Bible Gateway. https://www.biblegateway.com/passage/?search=Jeremiah%2033%3A10-11&version=NIV

22. Wimer, R. (2022, June 13). *A Galilean wedding*. Robert Wimer. https://robertwimer.com/a-galilean-wedding/
23. *Matthew 25:6-7 (NIV)*. (n.d.). Bible Gateway. https://www.biblegateway.com/passage/?search=Matthew%2025%3A6-7&version=NIV
24. *Matthew 7:16 & 21 (NIV)*. (n.d.). Bible Gateway. https://www.biblegateway.com/passage/?search=Matthew%207%3A21&version=NIV
25. Kaufman, M. (2017, July 6). *The chuppah, or wedding canopy*. My Jewish Learning. https://www.myjewishlearning.com/article/the-huppah-or-wedding-canopy/
26. *Proverbs 18:22 (NIV)*. (n.d.). Bible Gateway. https://www.biblegateway.com/passage/?search=Proverbs%2018%3A22&version=NIV
27. *John 14:3 (NIV)*. (n.d.). Bible Gateway. https://www.biblegateway.com/passage/?search=John%2014%3A3&version=NIV
28. Kagan, D. (2024, September 30). *Kiddushin — Step by step*. המסורת היהודית. https://yahadut.org/en/family/the-wedding/kiddushin-step-by-step-1/
29. *John 2:1-12 (NIV)*. (n.d.). Bible Gateway. https://www.biblegateway.com/passage/?search=John%202%3A1-12&version=NIV
30. *John 15:5 (NIV)*. (n.d.). Bible Gateway. https://www.biblegateway.com/passage/?search=John%2015%3A5&version=NIV
31. *Ancient Jewish wedding customs and Yeshua's second Coming | Messianic Bible*. (2022, April 27). Messianic Bible. https://www.messianicbible.com/feature/ancient-jewish-wedding-customs-and-yeshuas-second-coming/
32. *Song of Songs 2:15 (NIV)*. (n.d.). Bible Gateway. https://www.biblegateway.com/passage/?search=Song%20of%20Songs%202%3A15&version=NIV

33. *1 Corinthians 13:1-2 (NIV). (n.d.). Bible Gateway.* https://www.biblegateway.com/passage/?search=1%20Corinthians%2013%3A1-2&version=NIV
34. *Psalm 24:1 (NKJV). (n.d.). Bible Gateway.* https://www.biblegateway.com/passage/?search=psalm%2024%3A1&version=NKJV
35. *Proverbs 6:1-5 (NKJV). (n.d.). Bible Gateway.* https://www.biblegateway.com/passage/?search=Proverbs%206%3A1-5&version=NKJV
36. *Ephesians 5:21-22; 25 (NKJV). (n.d.). Bible Gateway.* https://www.biblegateway.com/passage/?search=Ephesians%205%3A21&version=NKJV
37. *1 Timothy 6:10; 17-19 (NKJV). (n.d.). Bible Gateway.* https://www.biblegateway.com/passage/?search=1%20Timothy%206%3A10%3B%2017-19&version=NKJV
38. *Proverbs 22:7 (ESV). (n.d.). Bible Gateway.* https://www.biblegateway.com/passage/?search=Proverbs%2022%3A7&version=ESV
39. *Leviticus 27:30 (NKJV). (n.d.). Bible Gateway.* https://www.biblegateway.com/passage/?search=Leviticus%2027%3A30&version=NKJV
40. *2 Corinthians 9:7-8 (NKJV). (n.d.). Bible Gateway.* https://www.biblegateway.com/passage/?search=2%20Corinthians%209%3A7-8&version=NKJV
41. *James 4:1 (NASB). (n.d.). Bible Gateway.* https://www.biblegateway.com/passage/?search=James%204%3A1&version=NASB
42. *Psalm 119:11 (NIV). (n.d.). Bible Gateway.* https://www.biblegateway.com/passage/?search=Psalm%20119%3A11&version=NIV
43. *Joshua 24:15 (NIV). (n.d.). Bible Gateway.* https://www.biblegateway.com/passage/?search=Joshua%2024%3A15&version=NIV

44. *Song of Songs 6:3 (NIV)*. (n.d.). Bible Gateway. https://www.biblegateway.com/passage/?search=Song%20of%20Songs%206%3A3&version=NIV
45. *1 Corinthians 6:17-20 (NIV)*. (n.d.). Bible Gateway. https://www.biblegateway.com/passage/?search=1%20Corinthians%206%3A17-20&version=NIV
46. Mitchell, T., & Mitchell, T. (2024, April 14). *Marriage and cohabitation in the U.S.* Pew Research Center. https://www.pewresearch.org/social-trends/2019/11/06/marriage-and-cohabitation-in-the-u-s/
47. Stanton, G. T. (2025, February 10). *Mapping US unmarried cohabitation rates.* Daily Citizen. https://dailycitizen.focusonthefamily.com/mapping-us-unmarried-cohabitation-rates/
48. Manning, W. D., Longmore, M. A., & Giordano, P. C. (2016). *Cohabitation and intimate partner violence during emerging adulthood: high constraints and low commitment.* Journal of Family Issues, 39(4), 1030—1055. https://doi.org/10.1177/0192513x16686132
49. *1 Corinthians 13:3-8 (NKJV)*. (n.d.). Bible Gateway. https://www.biblegateway.com/passage/?search=1%20Corinthians%2013%3A3-8&version=NKJV
50. *Luke 22:14-20 (ESV)*. (n.d.). Bible Gateway. https://www.biblegateway.com/passage/?search=Luke%2022%3A14-20&version=ESV
51. *Matthew 5:23-25 (NIV)*. (n.d.). Bible Gateway. https://www.biblegateway.com/passage/?search=Matthew%205%3A23-25&version=NIV
52. *1 Timothy 5:8 (NIV)*. (n.d.). Bible Gateway. https://www.biblegateway.com/passage/?search=1%20Timothy%205%3A8&version=NIV
53. *Matthew 18:21-35 (NKJV)*. (n.d.). Bible Gateway. https://www.biblegateway.com/passage/?search=Matthew%2018%3A21-35&version=NKJV

54. Loveing, M. (2025, February 4). Hooked: The bonding Power of sex. *FamilyLife - a Cru Ministry*. https://www.familylife.com/articles/topics/parenting/parenting-challenges/sexual-wholeness/hooked-the-bonding-power-of-sex/#:~:text=Another%20thing%20teens%20may%20not,addicted%2C%20bonded%20to%20each%20other.
55. *James 4:7 (NIV)*. (n.d.). Bible Gateway. https://www.biblegateway.com/passage/?search=James%204%3A7&version=NIV
56. *1 Thessalonians 4:3-7 (NIV)*. (n.d.). Bible Gateway. https://www.biblegateway.com/passage/?search=1%20Thessalonians%204%3A3-7&version=NIV
57. *Song of Solomon 4:6-7 (MSG)*. (n.d.). Bible Gateway. https://www.biblegateway.com/passage/?search=Song%20of%20Songs%204%3A6-7&version=MSG
58. *Proverbs 5:18-19 (NIV)*. (n.d.). Bible Gateway. https://www.biblegateway.com/passage/?search=%20Proverbs%205%3A18-19&version=NIV
59. *Hebrews 13:4 (NIV)*. (n.d.). Bible Gateway. https://www.biblegateway.com/passage/?search=Hebrews%2013%3A4&version=NIV
60. *Philippians 1:6 (ESV)*. (n.d.). Bible Gateway. https://www.biblegateway.com/passage/?search=Philippians%201%3A6&version=ESV

Made in the USA
Coppell, TX
23 February 2026

72127275R00184

## From the author who brought you *Break Free*...

You've had the wedding, said the vows, and now you're in the real thing. But contrary to what we see in movies and TV shows, marriage is not always "flowers and rainbows". For many, they would say they are doing pretty well, while others find themselves in misery. But it doesn't have to be that way.

*I Still Do* is a resource for married couples of all age ranges and longevity, whether you've just said "I do," or you've been "I-doing" for several decades. Marriage is a beautiful gift from God, the only relationship that God ordained as a picture of what an intimate relationship with Him is supposed to look like. But so often, the enemy comes in and wreaks havoc in our marriage relationships by bringing division and hardship. How do we walk through hardships and not allow them to break us, but rather strengthen us?

In this 18-chapter resource, you will be challenged with deep dives into topics including Covenant, Communication, and Biblical Sexuality. Satan is after the family, and its breakdown is one of his highest goals. But God is all about restoration, and His main goal is to see His people living life to the fullest, with relationships that thrive, in and through His Spirit. Each chapter deals with a specific hardship or place of "tune-up" for your marriage and how you can strengthen potential areas of weakness. At the end of each chapter, you will find Marriage Activations meant to bring you and your spouse closer and make your marriage stronger than ever!

## Throughout this book, you will:

- Learn God's original intent for the marriage relationship as you study His Word

- Transform your understanding and appreciation for your spouse and how God sees them

- Cultivate a life of prayer with your spouse, thus building a strong foundation for your relationship and home

It is never too late, and no marriage is too far gone that God cannot restore. Purpose to dig deep and do the work of revolutionizing your relationship, and reap the benefits of a God-centered marriage!

James Boyd is passionate about seeing marriages not only last, but thrive! With over thirty years of marriage and family counseling experience, he longs to see people walk in the freedom and wonder that only a marriage can bring. He has been married to his wonderful wife, Charlene, for thirty-five years and has two children and four grandchildren. James is the Lead Pastor of Refuge City Church in Klamath Falls, Oregon.

ISBN 9798990487222